TIME TRAVEL DINOSAUR

MATT YOUNGMARK

TIME TRAVEL DINOSAUR

With illustrations
by the author

CHOOSEOMATIC BOOKS, SEATTLE

An imprint of Atherton Haight

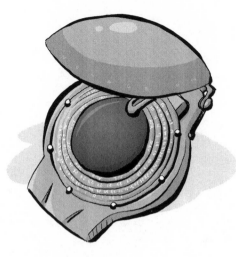

Second edition, September 2015

atherton
HAIGHT

Chooseomatic Books and the Chooseomatic Books and
Atherton Haight logos are registered trademarks of Atherton Haight.

www.chooseomatic.com

Illustrations by Matt Youngmark

Library of Congress Cataloging-In-Publication Data
is available on request.

ISBN 13: 978-0-9840678-8-6
ISBN 10: 0-9840678-8-4

You find yourself lying chin-down on a threadbare rug in an unfamiliar room. Slowly, the fog in your head starts to lift. You glance around to see a bearded, wild-eyed man with about twenty pounds of cobbled-together machinery strapped to his chest. He's working at a whiteboard frantically, rubbing out sections with his fist and filling in new numbers with a dry-erase marker. The year, if everything has gone as planned, should be 1983. And it's a pretty safe bet that this guy is your mission objective.

Your ears perk up and you absentmindedly scratch your neck with a hind leg. We should mention at this point that you're currently inhabiting the body of a Labrador retriever.

The Time Travel Investigation Agency might sound like an exciting place to work, but you've learned that the actual business of time travel investigation is unbelievably dull. There

(continue to the next page)

are several hard-and-fast physical laws that govern time travel, and those laws tend to make quantum exploration a remarkably boring affair.

First: you can't travel to any period before November 5, 1931—presumably the date that time travel was invented. This puts some fairly severe limits on time travel as a means to clarify the historical record. You also can't visit any date after August 12, 2271, although nobody knows why (no investigator who looked into it has ever returned to file a report, which tends to discourage further study).

Second: you can't send physical matter through time, so your actual body doesn't make the trip. You can only transfer your consciousness into a body that already exists in the targeted time period—it's called the Bakula Principle. If your own body is alive and well at whatever age, you'll automatically snap into it, but if you travel before your birth or after your death, you can float around a bit and select a convenient host. Which explains the Labrador retriever. It also explains how a recent college graduate like yourself got hired as a Time Travel Investigator—the fewer years you've been alive, the more years you have to travel the timestream freely without being pulled into a younger version of yourself.

Third: the whole idea that you can alter the past is a fantasy, since alternate timestreams would break Einstein's theory of relativity. There's only one reality, so if you travel back in time and accomplish anything at all, that action is already part of history before you get there. Your boss, Professor Venkataraman, insists that this doesn't necessarily prove all human decisions are predestined, but the subtleties are lost on you. What it definitely

(continue to the next page)

means is that no one can go back in time and stop Hitler (though *many* have tried) or accidentally screw up the past.

All of this, in turn, would seem to mean that your job is largely pointless.

In fact, all you really do is visit miscellaneous crackpots between the years of 1931 and 1990 and verify that they aren't involved in miscellaneous time travel shenanigans. Spoiler alert: they never are. Sure, the Agency will occasionally discover a rare case where some joker manages to travel back and feed himself winning lottery numbers, and then retroactively build a time machine with the winnings. But you have yet to uncover anything like that, and if your luck holds out, you never will. The paperwork required to report self-inducing chronology loop is *mind-boggling.*

As you observe your mark, you're increasingly convinced that you have nothing to worry about. He seems intent on giving his dog a play-by-play description of everything he's doing, which is making your job remarkably easy. He also seems to be under the impression that his dog is a government spy, which is making your job *hilarious.*

"This is it, Betsy," he says, vaguely gesturing at a digital clock on his chest that looks like it was yanked from the dashboard of an Oldsmobile. "In exactly one minute, the fabric of the universe will tear open, and I'll remove myself from the space-time continuum completely!"

Yeah, this guy's nuts. You start making the mental preparations to terminate the mission and transfer your consciousness back to the present day. Meanwhile, Mad Science Guy continues to rant.

(continue to the next page)

"Tell them I did it, Betsy!" The timer on his chest is at 45 seconds. "Tell your secret masters that I have conquered reality itself! By the time you—"

Before he can finish, a shimmering blue portal appears in the air behind him. An exact duplicate of the scientist leaps out of it holding what looks to be an antique revolver, and shoots the original version right in the face.

What. The. Fuuuuuuuuuu…

The portal collapses shut, and the second scientist flashes you a grin, cackling wildly. He fiddles with a dial on his chest rig and opens up a new portal that he dives into, leaving you alone with the corpse of his alternate self.

You're not entirely sure what you just witnessed—did this guy just break all the unbreakable laws of quantum mechanics? Physically traveling through time, killing his past self—that's at *least* two. You need a moment to process all this, but you realize that, if the second portal closes as quickly as the first one did, you don't have that moment to spare.

Then again, you're pretty much *in a dog* at the moment. What can you possibly hope to accomplish by chasing after him?

▶ *If you jump into the portal and pursue the scientist,* **turn to page 7.**

▶ *If you immediately report back to your superiors at the Time Travel Investigation Agency,* **turn to page 9.**

You set off to find some nineteenth century ruffians, which turns out to be harder than you'd think. In fact, it's past sunset when you finally stumble across a band of thugs, each of whom has at least one limb made of clockwork machinery. They're tinkering with what looks like some kind of huge, steampunk surface-to-air missile, built out of copper and brass.

Their leader is a particularly ugly specimen with two arms and one leg all steampunked out. As you approach, the goons form a circle around you.

"You got nerve showing yourself 'round these parts, mutton shunter," the leader says. You're not sure you even want to *know* what a mutton shunter is.

Chance is unintimidated. "Horse! I've got business with your boss, my friend." His jaw tightens. "So tell me who's giving orders around here, and no one needs to get hurt, yes?"

The thug—"Horse," apparently—just sneers. "Things have changed since last time you was here. *We're* the cops now. So hands on yer heads, nice and easy."

He gives you a stare that could wilt lettuce. "You too, lizard puss. Boss mighta' said to leave you be, but that was before you showed up with this plonker."

Chance catches your eye and gives you a little nod. Wait, what does that even *mean*? Is he signaling you to attack? Or to let yourself be captured, so they'll take you to whoever's in charge?

▶ *If you assume that Chance has your back and spring into action,* **turn to page 162.**

▶ *If you think he's planning subterfuge and let the thugs restrain you,* **turn to page 30.**

"None of this is real!" you say. "I'm mostly stuck to the fabric of the universe, but a tiny part of me is peeled off! That's why the world keeps going crazy!" You unscrew your eyes and realize that the universe has shifted again, and you're back in the operating room.

There's no turning back now, though. "I need to travel back in time and murder myself in the past! It's the only way out!" Your Labrador-headed surgical assistants call security, and you try even harder to explain your predicament to the orderlies as they haul you off. Fortunately, this hospital has a well-funded psychiatric wing.

It might be the last few tachyons fading away or the mind-boggling quantity of drugs they pump into you, but you finally stop shifting in and out of reality. You never let the doctors convince you that you're not a time traveler from another universe, though. One evening you're strapped into your bed after a particularly violent outburst, and you see a vision appear above you.

It's a gold watch with red and green lights mounted on top and a circular screen in the center. Wordlessly, it tells you that you've been chosen to travel the timeline, righting wrongs throughout history. Is this just a fantasy created by your poor, broken mind to distract you from your miserable fate?

Either way, you'll take it. You spend the rest of your days having wild adventures throughout time and space, and when your time finally comes, you pass the watch on to an enthusiastic gentleman named Boris who continues your noble legacy.

If it was all a dream, it was a lovely one.

THE END

This is no time to hesitate! You plunge into the rift and find yourself hurtling through the fabric of reality. The fabric of reality, it turns out, looks more or less like cheap CGI. You drift weightlessly through a tunnel of psychedelic light, then pop out the other side with a jolt. The unexpected impact of re-entering the timestream knocks you right out of the Labrador retriever.

Crap! Usually when you make a timejump, your consciousness gently floats around until you either find a host or, failing that, you slip back to your own time period and try again. This time, however, everything feels wrong. The subtle mental link you should have with your native time period is completely missing. As your awareness drifts upward, you see Betsy the dog running toward a thicket of odd-looking palm trees.

The enormous, leathery form of a Tyrannosaurus rex promptly crashes out of the tree line.

Okay, that would mean you're way, *way* further back than 1931, and the third unbreakable law of time travel has snapped like a twig. Also, that dinosaur is totally going to eat that dog. You have to save Betsy!

Or do you? She doesn't belong in this era, and all laws of time and space seem to have gone out the window. Is it safe to leave a Labrador wandering around the Cretaceous period?

▶ *If you transfer your consciousness back into the dog and help her escape,* **turn to page 16**.

▶ *If you transfer your consciousness into the T. rex,* **turn to page 34**.

▶ *If you let whatever's going to happen here happen and look for a different host altogether (like, duh, the mad scientist),* **turn to page 112**.

The 1880s were reasonably boring, right? What's the worst thing that could happen to you there? Professor Velociraptor shows you which button to push on your wrist device and how to return to your own time when you're done. After a quick hop through a shimmering portal and a brief period weightlessly drifting through Laser Floyd, you find yourself in a dingy alley in the rain.

"Warning! Emergency curfew in effect! All citizenry restricted to housing!"

You jump about a foot into the air, then realize that the loud, mechanical voice isn't directed at you. Peeking around the corner, you spot a pair of children on the cobblestone street. Approaching them is some kind of motorized policeman, eight feet tall and built of iron with gears spinning and a jet of steam venting from a pipe on the top of its head.

Something's screwy here. History was never your strong suit, but you're almost positive that there shouldn't be robots in this century. The children cower in fear—you can't see them clearly from this distance, but based on their size, they can't be older than eight or ten—and the automaton raises its billy club as if preparing to strike.

Whoa. Not cool, steamcop.

▶ *If you intervene,* **turn to page 73.**

▶ *If you stay hidden and observe (I mean, for all you know they could be TERRORIST eight-year-old children),* **turn to page 238.**

You've completed dozens of missions for the TTIA, but the return trip has never felt like this. Something is horribly wrong—the gentle, tingly sensation you're accustomed to has been replaced by a gut-wrenching vertigo. It finally subsides, and you open your eyes. Rather than the serene face of Professor Venkataraman, you're greeted by a terrifying human-sized lizard creature with a mouth full of razor-sharp teeth.

It's wearing a lab coat.

You scream. (You're not proud of that, but hey, it felt right at the time.) But as you look into the creature's ridged, yellow eyes, memories start flooding back. *Venkataraman?* Where did *that* come from? Of course this is your boss, Professor Velociraptor. You've worked with her just about every day for the past six months.

Your scream peters out into a sort of questioning grunt. Professor V. grabs you by the shoulders. "Is it a lottery winner? It's okay! I can help with the paperwork!"

You attempt to describe the horrific scene you've just witnessed—shimmering portals, face-murder, interior design trends of the early 1980s—but get stuck describing the scientist himself. "I want to say he had a... *beard*?" That can't be right. Dinofolk don't have monkey hair growing out of their faces. "Like, he was maybe some sort of ape-creature?" You feel like that information should have seemed more important at the time. As you try to remember him, though, the scientist's features become even less clear in your mind.

"Oh, no," Professor Velociraptor says. "I was afraid of something like this. Come with me—quickly!"

She leads you to the back of the lab and punches some

(continue to the next page)

numbers into a keypad on the wall, which splits open to reveal a secret chamber. "Everything I've taught you about time travel is true," she says. "At least, as far as Bakulan theory is concerned. But I've been studying a second, non-Bakulan time travel method which dispenses with those rules. Physical transfer, limitless date access, causality paradoxes—it's all possible. And it's unbelievably dangerous."

You stare at her blankly for a moment. "Then why do we even *bother* with the Bakula stuff?"

"Oh," she says, fiddling with a glowing piece of equipment on a stainless steel workbench. The tech on this side of the secret door, incidentally, looks *way* cooler than the junk in the other room. "For the lottery winners. We get a cut every time someone has to return their winnings due to time travel fraud. It makes up 95 percent of our funding."

She finishes tinkering and holds the device in front of her. It's a chunky wristband, a little too big to fit comfortably on your… *tiny little arms*? You look down, not sure why for a moment you were expecting them to be bigger. You're a tyrannoid, which means small arms, a big head, and a powerful tail that makes it incredibly hard to find decent-fitting clothes. Due to convergent evolution, the various species of dinofolk have shrunk or grown to approximately equal size (and of course, they all walk upright, even the Brachiosaurs), but other than that, they've retained the same basic characteristics since prehistoric times. That's just science.

"The subject has clearly stumbled upon non-Bakulan time travel," Professor V. says, "and if your memories are getting hazy, it may mean he's already made changes to the timestream. The

(continue to the next page)

trouble is, there's no way to know what he changed because our memories would have changed right along with it."

"Then how can we stop him if we don't even know what to stop?"

"*We* don't stop him," she says. "*You* do. And you do it by following his lead: you must create a paradox so drastic that it peels you off the space-time continuum entirely. Then no matter what happens to the timestream, you'll retain your own personal history and memories."

You're having a hard time processing all of this. "Me? I make *eleven bucks an hour*. Wouldn't someone else be more qualified?"

"I can't do it myself," she says. "I'm one of the inventors of this device, which means tachyon particles affect me unpredictably. It wouldn't be safe." She attaches the glowing bracelet to your wrist. Then she places a cold, heavy pistol into your palm.

"I'm sending you one minute back in time to kill the version of yourself you find there. I know it sounds extreme, but trust me. It's the only way to stop this madman."

▶ *Sure! What's a little murder between time-shifted alternate selves? If you tell Professor Velociraptor you're in,* **turn to page 12.**

▶ *Whoa, whoa, whoa. If you refuse to murder anyone, least of all yourself,* **turn to page 14.**

Professor Velociraptor is a good boss, and you've always liked her. She gave you that extra day off after you got super drunk at the Halloween party. You can trust her when she tells you to go back in time and murder yourself, right?

"You're going to pop out directly behind your other self," she says. You feel a sharp pang of déjà vu as she's talking but shrug it off. "Make it quick and clean, because the universe is going to do its best to auto-correct. If you're only wounded, you might survive long enough to make the jump back again, and…"

She trails off. "Just get the job done. It has to be drastic, and it has to be fast if this is going to work."

Gulp. Okay, you can do this. Gun training wasn't part of your two-week time travel preparedness course, but a point-blank shot to the back of the head should do the trick, right? Professor V. presses a button of your armband, and a shimmering blue portal appears in front of you.

You hold your breath and leap into it. When you emerge on the other side, you get an odd sense of altered perspective from appearing in a different spot in the same room. You see yourself from behind—wow, does your tail always look that big?—talking to the Professor. The alternate you hears your feet hit the floor and starts to turn around, startled.

This is it.

▶ *Fire! If you go for the kill shot,* **turn to page 17.**

▶ *No! If you can't bear to do it and chicken out,* **turn to page 24.**

Such stubbornness! Such determination! You push forward until you spot the mad scientist making his way through the vegetation, away from the rampaging T. rex. (He may be insane, but he's not *suicidal*). It's like trying to dog paddle through molasses, but you float as hard as you can toward him. Your consciousness starts to go fuzzy. Uh oh. Just a little farther! Almost there…

Almost… *there…*

Bingo! You overtake the scientist and wedge yourself into his cranium. What you find inside, however, is deeply upsetting. His mind is a jumble of contradicting memories with huge, empty swaths where basic brain functions should be and a central core of utter rage. Worst of all, though? *He knows you're in there.*

You! he thinks angrily. *How could you have followed me?* He makes a little mental gasping sound. *Of course! You steered Betsy through the portal! But combining corporeal and non-corporeal time travel would mean… That's it! I can mix the two methods to break through the barriers of causality! It would take time and power… SO MUCH POWER…*

He descends into a fit of maniacal laughter, ejecting your consciousness from his mind through sheer force of will. In your weakened state, there's no hope of finding another host before you dissipate entirely. You fade away to nothingness, but not before giving your nemesis the very idea he needs to completely shatter the fabric of the multiverse.

You damn, stubborn fool.

The End

"I just can't do it," you say. The truth is, you're not sure you understand all this business with paradoxes in the timestream. But it seems like it has the potential to get SERIOUSLY nuts, and you figure if you're going to draw the line anywhere, it might as well be murdering alternate versions of yourself.

Professor Velociraptor sighs. "I understand. Perhaps I can find someone else for this mission. Sit right here while I make some phone calls—you're still temporally linked to the original timestream, so I'll still need you to…"

She keeps talking, but you're suddenly overcome with an all-too-familiar, gut-wrenching vertigo. Crap! Whatever that peeling-yourself-off-the-fabric-of-reality business was, you've opted out. Is this what happens when someone messes with the timestream?

The room spins around you, and Professor V.'s voice is replaced by that of a panicked young man. You open your eyes to discover what looks like an operating room.

"He's crashing!" the young man says. The first thing you notice is that he's dressed in green scrubs. The second is that, under his surgical mask, he seems to have the head of a dog. In fact, you realize that everyone in this room is covered in fur as if they had evolved from Labrador retrievers.

"What do we do, Doctor?" another voice asks. Everyone's looking at you. Are *you* the doctor? Just a moment ago, you were in an entirely different room with… *a talking dinosaur?* Eight years of medical school come rushing back. How is it even possible that you had eight years of medical school when you're only 22? Is this some sort of Doogie Howser thing?

Is it… *Doggie* Howser?

(continue to the next page)

Perhaps that isn't what you should focus on right now. You look down and see a patient spread out on a gurney with a gaping hole in his torso. Open heart surgery? No, it's lower than that. Open liver surgery? Is that even a thing? Wait, now you remember! It's an appendectomy!

"Doctor!" one of your assistants says with more than a little panic in her voice. You're not sure why your head is so foggy, but you're a surgeon, damnit. And if you want to save this patient's life, you have to act fast.

▶ *If you tell them to yank that man's appendix out of him, pronto,* **turn to page 266.**

▶ *If you call for 50 cc of magnesium sulphate, STAT,* **turn to page 138.**

Betsy's a good dog—after having access to her innermost thoughts and feelings, you can make that judgement comprehensively—and you'll be damned if you're going to let her wind up as a snack for some Jurassic reject. (Technically you're in the Cretaceous period, which along with the Jurassic and Triassic form the Mesozoic era, but this is no time for paleontology, damnit. You've got a dog to rescue!)

You settle back into the familiar environs of the Labrador retriever, which would be nice and cozy if it weren't for the overwhelming sense of abject terror. You spot a clump of low bushes that might offer some cover, but it's on the far side of seven tons of apex predator. Is there any chance you could get past the thing? I mean, something that huge can't be terribly maneuverable, right?

Behind you is nothing but open plains and a nasty-looking prehistoric river. If you run your little canine legs off, you might make it there before the T. rex runs you down. To be honest, though, you're not sure your chances of survival are any higher in the raging rapids. But at least the water doesn't have *nine inch teeth.*

▶ *If you run toward the river and hurl yourself in,*
   turn to page 50.

▶ *If you try to scoot past the dinosaur and find safety in the shrubbery,* **turn to page 82.**

You pull the trigger and are treated to the truly horrifying experience of witnessing your own violent death. Meanwhile, every fiber of your being feels like it's being torn apart on a molecular level. Being peeled off of the space-time continuum, it turns out, is no picnic. You're overcome by a flood of vivid memories from throughout your life—graduations, birthdays, first kisses, and predictably awkward first sexual experiences. You realize that they belong to you alone now, and the other people featured in them may wind up remembering them very differently.

In fact, for all you know, those people may no longer even exist.

You glance over at Professor V., who in turn is staring at the dead body on her laboratory floor. "For some reason, I assumed it would disappear into the timestream or something," she says.

You step backward, realizing that the expanding pool of blood is about to reach your toes. "Yeah," you say awkwardly. "It's not disappearing."

"No."

At least the sight of your lifeless, bleeding doppelganger is keeping your mind off of the existential dread that comes from not truly belonging anywhere in space-time. You hear a soft pop behind you, followed by a gentle, almost musical voice.

"Professor Velociraptor? I... oh, my. I've caught you at a bad time, haven't I?" You turn to see a woman with the head of a dolphin dressed in some kind of skin-tight space suit. Just standing there.

"This must be your initial paradox incident," she says, squinting at you, then at the dead duplicate on the floor. "That

(continue to the next page)

is traumatizing, isn't it?" She gives you a compassionate look that's oddly soulful despite her beady little dolphin eyes. "I'm so sorry."

"Um, thanks?" You're not quite sure how to accept condolences from a talking dolphin. "Do I know you?"

"Not yet, I think," she says. "Professor Velociraptor, I need your help. I've come from the Cretaceous period, where we're attempting to build a tachyon shield and prevent a worldwide extinction event. By all accounts, you're the only person who can help."

"Me?" Professor V. says, taken aback. "You must be mistaken. I'm not even sure what a tachyon shield *is*."

"Hmm. Perhaps I've come too early. I apologize for the intrusion. Please continue with whatever you were doing as if I was never here."

"Wait," you say. "What we're doing is trying to stop some crazy monkey guy from destroying the timeline. Sounds like maybe I should head for the Cretaceous period?"

"No, if you've only just peeled off, you have quite a bit to do before that," she says. "Trust me." Again with the soulful dolphin eyes. How does she even *do* that?

There's another pop, and the woman disappears. "Okay, that was weird," you say.

"Indeed," Professor V. says, tapping her chin with one claw. "Nevertheless, we've got work to do."

She leads you to a computer screen (which, with your limited comprehension of quantum physics, looks more like the old arcade game *Tempest* than anything else) and explains that it's displaying spikes in temporal activity throughout time

(continue to the next page)

and space. Apparently at this stage, there's no stopping the mad scientist from conducting his experiment—since he's no longer bound by linear causality, you could prevent him from ever being born, and he'd still be out there in the timestream messing stuff up. Your only chance is to find out what he's up to and straight-up thwart his ass.

Professor V. tells you that she's found traces of your tachyon signature—which, theoretically, should match the scientist's—amid three major Temporal Activity Clusters throughout history. These clusters indicate an abundance of time travel events, and she thinks that you should start by investigating one of them.

The first is more than two and a half centuries in the future, on the exact date in 2271 that no agent has ever traveled past. The second is in the early 1880s. And the third, just as the dolphin suggested, is in the late Cretaceous period. She seemed to be steering you away from that era, but can you really trust random sea animals that appear out of thin air?

"Remember," Professor V. says, "no matter what happens out there, your mission is to protect the *real* timeline. *Our* timeline." She puts one hand on your shoulder and looks you straight in the eyes.

"The timeline where people evolved from *dinosaurs*."

▶ *If you head for the Cretaceous (talking dolphins aren't the boss of you!),* **turn to page 48.**

▶ *If you investigate the distant future,* **turn to page 63.**

▶ *If you think the 1880s are your best bet,* **turn to page 8.**

You've been handed a golden opportunity to get some royal facetime and intend to make the most of it. You know, *murder-wise.* Fleck insists on accompanying you, and her father somehow manages to give his permission and a fairly lengthy safety lecture without specifying the child's gender. You've been hanging out with this kid WAY too long to bring it up at this point, but you've settled on thinking of Fleck as a "her with an asterisk." If she ever decides to present herself as either male or female, you figure you'll just roll with it.

You set out at some absurd pre-dawn hour for the capital city—seriously, with modern transportation it would be like a 45-minute trip—and arrive just in time to be escorted to the king's chambers for your audience by a phalanx of guards. They take your weapons first, which is disconcerting if not completely unexpected.

(continue to the next page)

You bend over to whisper in Boris's ear on the way in. "So we do this thing, then you whisk us all away into the timestream, right? That's the plan?"

"What? No, the stopwatch can only transport *me*," he whispers back. He has the watch open, and you catch a glimpse of chaos and swords and… blood, maybe? "I'm sorry, didn't I make that clear? You do have your own time travel device, don't you?"

Uh oh. You're ushered into a huge, gaudy chamber with a throne right in the middle. The man sitting on it is small and portly, his belly extruding from beneath his exquisitely crafted robes. One of his eyes is weirdly pale and stares off to the left, and his scraggly beard is caked with what must be several days worth of food.

Trumpets flare. "Your royal majesty," a slightly terrified looking aide says, "I present the Cursed Demon Lord of the Eastern Mud Flats."

"Graaah!" the king screeches, not to anyone in particular but just out to the room in general. "What gifts does this lord bring to prove his devotion to the crown?"

Crud, were you supposed to bring gifts? Fleck takes a half-step forward. "We've doubled our monthly production in honor of your boundless wisdom and generosity, my liege," she says.

"Good, good," the king mutters. "But it isn't enough. Triple it! Quadruple it! The glory of the realm demands four times as much… uh…"

"Mud, Your Highness," his aide says.

"Whatever! All of it! All the mud! Bring it all to me!"

Fleck's little jaw stiffens. "Many of our people would suffer greatly, perhaps even work themselves to death in an attempt to

(continue to the next page)

harvest so much, Your Majesty."

"Then they suffer for their king!" he says. "They die for the glory of the realm! What greater aspiration could the contemptible peasantry aspire to?" He slouches off of his throne and approaches you, drawing close until his face is inches away from yours. "Your Lord and Sovereign, hand of the Almighty Himself, demands it!" he howls. Needless to say, you get coated in spittle. "Kneel, demon, and swear your allegiance to the crown!"

You glance at Boris, but he seems utterly befuddled. Fleck, on the other hand, is almost shaking with rage. She catches your eye and makes a tiny biting gesture with her mouth.

Is she suggesting that you…? *Ewww.* Granted, these mammal-folk have heads much smaller than yours, and as a tyrannoid, you do have a powerful jaw and a set of truly magnificent teeth. But the idea of chewing on another person—and particularly this vile creature—is utterly repellent to you. Still, if any king ever deserved a little regicide, it's this one. You don't know if his death would make life any better for Fleck and her people, but you're pretty sure it couldn't make things worse.

"Your Majesty," the king's aide says, interrupting. "When you're finished here, the royal magician has requested an audience with the demon lord."

Royal magician? That sounds interesting. The king glares at you. If you're going to do something, you'd better do it now.

▶ *Screw it. If you bite the little bastard's head off,* **turn to page 197.**

▶ *If you kneel, swear loyalty, and go see what the royal magician wants,* **turn to page 249.**

You've literally *never* seen a hole in the fabric of time and space that you didn't immediately chuck yourself into. Alas, this time it isn't meant to be. The robosaur has quicker reflexes than you do, and even though you make a sporty feint to the left before trying to blow past it on the right, it's no use.

Your adversary's teeth cut through your underbelly like warm butter, and it proceeds to chew up everything it finds inside. Just before you expire, you realize it's not actually trying to eat you but to dig out the time machine that's still embedded in your stomach. Granted, once it does, it immediately chews up and eats the time machine.

Robot dinosaurs: truly one of life's mysteries.

THE END

"There must be another way," you say, lowering your weapon. "Murdering some other version of myself can't possibly be the answer."

"Wait, what?" the other you says, bewildered.

"What if I just don't go through the portal this time?" you ask. "That's a paradox, isn't it?"

Professor Velociraptor frowns and shakes her head. "It has to be more severe than that. The universe will want to fix it. It'll find a way to work itself out."

"Yeah, I *really* feel like I should go through that time portal," the other you says. "How do I do it? Just push this button here?"

"No!" you shout as the shimmering vortex appears. You grab your other self by the arm. "We have to figure this out! If you go through, you'll have to kill me to make a paradox! Or I'll have to kill you, or…" Now you're getting confused. Is this going to make a third version of you show up? Your doppelganger tries to get free from your grasp, so you wrestle yourself to the floor and wind up tangled together in a big heap. You literally can't tell if the arm pushed up against the side of your face belongs to you or… *you.*

"I know it seems drastic, but you must do this to create an impossible eventuality in the timestream and peel yourself off the space-time continuum," Professor V. says.

Your doppelganger gives you a pathetic look, which you recognize as your "please do not murder me" face.

"Wait!" you say. "What if we destroy the time travel device?" There are now two copies of the time bracelet—one on your wrist and one on your alternate self's. If you destroy the other one, your double can't use it to make the time jump,

(continue to the next page)

become you, and destroy it in the first place. Paradox! It's a little convoluted, but it has to be a better option than self-murder.

"Brilliant!" the other version of you says. "We should totally do that! I'm in if you're in."

"Please don't," Professor Velociraptor says.

▶ *No, you're pretty sure this will work. If you go ahead and destroy the time travel bracelet,* **turn to page 94.**

▶ *If you listen to the professor and back off,* **turn to page 151.**

"Perhaps you're right," Krikri says. "You try to figure out what's going on here, and I'll continue my research into the past. I'll let you know if I turn anything up." With a pop she's gone, and suddenly, you feel very alone.

You walk into the empty streets to investigate and see Krikri a few blocks down, standing on a big pedestal, raising one hand as if trying to get your attention. She's back already? That was fast! As you start walking toward her, though, a futuristic motorcycle comes out of literally nowhere and almost runs you down.

A well-muscled man in a leather jacket dismounts from it. "Chance Bruxelles, Time Patrol," he says. "Time license and—wait. Damnit!"

You're a little taken aback by his introduction. "Captain Steele said I'd either be the first person to travel past August 12, 2271, or I'd explode," he continues. "But I survive, only to find *you* here?"

"I'm stranded," you say. "Could you maybe give me a lift back to my own time period?"

"Oh, no!" he says. "You got yourself here, you can get yourself out. Good day."

"But—"

"I said good day!"

He revs his motorcycle, preparing for a time jump. If you leap onto the back of his machine, you could still catch a ride out of here! It might be your only hope to ever escape 2271. He really does look pissed, though. Maybe you should just let him leave and go see what Krikri wants.

▶ If you try to piggyback on Chance's bike, turn to page 132.

▶ If you leave him be, turn to page 230.

If there's one thing you know about aristocratic steampunk dictators, it's that they're trustworthy. You let the sisters remove your bracelet and give them a quick lesson on its operation.

"Well, then," Cornelia says, gently turning her key in the little tech dampener that's been keeping you from using the device. "Let's see if this experience is everything they—"

Before she can finish, a time portal opens up behind her and a second Cornelia emerges, brandishing a long, curved knife. She stabs her duplicate in the back repeatedly, drowning out her own screams with a howl of glee.

"Beatrice, it's absolutely exhilarating!" she says, covered in her own blood as her doppelganger collapses to the floor "You *must* try it!"

Beatrice bends down to remove the bracelet from the dead sister's arm—hey, there are two time bracelets now, that's a neat trick—but before she does, a second Beatrice comes through a second portal and proceeds to murder her in a similarly brutal fashion. You note that there are three bracelets now, one for Cornelia, one for Beatrice, and one for—

Before you can finish the thought, a third pair of sisters emerges from a portal behind you, and you feel two blades plunge into your back.

Yeah, you probably should have seen that coming.

THE END

"Surrender" is a strong word. What you actually do is just stop moving, which at this point is *much* easier than the alternative. The automatons cease their attack and, once you've regained a reasonable amount of motor control, help you to your feet. (They're strong!) Hilariously, they also cuff your tiny T. rex arms together. Then they escort you across town to an industrial freight elevator that takes you deep into the bowels of the city.

At the bottom of the lift, you find a Japanese man dressed all in black and a platinum-haired woman with an expression that could cut glass. If she's surprised to see a Tyrannosaurus rex entering her basement, she doesn't let on.

"What's this?"

You're stooped low to fit inside the room, and the man reaches up and clamps a tiny clockwork contraption onto the side of your head. Suddenly, you lose every last bit of your recently-reclaimed bodily control. This time, however, your limbs remain stiff. The man taps each of your legs with his cane, and they lurch forward dutifully, regardless of any desires you might have to the contrary. He taps you on the snout, and your entire head lowers by several feet.

"It's a dinosaur," he says, just barely trying to hide his contempt. "Several species have been discovered already, even in this desolate century."

She looks you up and down, her eyes revealing nothing. "It's magnificent," she says at last. "Make me an army of them."

"Madame, I'm a *roboticist*, not a biologist. Even if I were *able* to replicate living systems—"

The woman cuts him off. "So make me a *robot* army of

(continue to the next page)

them. Prepare a list of needed materials, from any time period, and my sister will acquire them for you."

She makes her exit, and the man stares at you for a moment, as if considering the possibilities. Then he uses his cane to march you into an enormous steel chamber and throws a heavy switch on the wall. You instantaneously black out.

The chamber, it turns out, houses a time dilation field, which means that when you're inside it time doesn't pass at all. The roboticist thaws you out occasionally to run tests on various parts of your anatomy, but at no time during these sessions do you have much control over your primary motor functions. At some point they feed you a cow.

For all you know, the time between tests could be days, weeks, or even years. After twenty or thirty of them, however, something goes wrong. Rather than waking weightless and still suspended in the field, you collapse to the floor with a thud. The impact dislodges the motor inhibitor doohickey from your head. The chamber's doors are still shut, but you hear voices outside.

"Damnit, Chance," one of them says. It sounds vaguely familiar. "Stop flipping switches at random!"

"Aw, you worry too much." This one sounds like some action hero from the 1980s whose muscles are impressive enough that no one bothers to hire him a dialog coach. "What's the worst that could happen?"

The absolute worst? Well, you suppose that would be *you*.

▶ *If you barge out of the stasis chamber and attack,* **turn to page 42.**

▶ *If you refrain from making any hasty decisions, hoping to get a better sense of whatever's going on before you spring into action,* **turn to page 102.**

If Chance wants to bust some wild karate moves and take out all twelve of these guys at once, he's certainly free to do so. But you're a lover, not a fighter. Well, technically more of a surrenderer than a lover. But *definitely* not a fighter.

The steampunk ruffians are unable to make your tiny dinosaur arms reach behind your back for proper handcuffing, but they do tie your jaws shut to prevent you from biting anyone. Then they pat you down for technology and escort you inside

(continue to the next page)

the building they've been loitering in front of. As they do, Chance just smiles. Apparently that was a "let's get ourselves captured on purpose" nod after all.

Your captors drag you down a hallway and into a room where two elegantly dressed women are barking orders at various henchmen. The darker-haired one spots you first.

"Cornelia, the lizard thing's returned!" she says. "But whatever has happened to your magnificent hat?" She glares at your wrist with narrowing eyes. "And, more importantly, where has your time-hopping mechanism gotten off to?"

"Relax, Beatrice." The goons tighten their hold as the lighter-haired woman approaches for a closer inspection. "I think this visitor is *slightly* distinct from the one we entertained previously," she says. "Enlisted in the Time Patrol, have we? Tell me, do you hail from a date before our little chat or after?"

She flashes a smile, not quite able to contain her glee. "Or have you come to us from a separate chronology altogether?"

"Ha," Chance says. "Shows how smart you are. If we were from a different chronology, we'd be talking to a different *you*. The streams do not cross. Even *I* know this."

"Ah, but don't they? The fabric of creation is not as rugged as you believe, *patrolman*." She enunciates the last word with particular relish. "And if it's begun to tear, it can only mean our moment has finally come."

Suddenly, a streak of darkness appears in mid-air across the room. Huh. That certainly *looks* like a tear in the fabric of creation. A gnarled, shadowy figure pops its head through the rift and lets out a terrifying screech.

"That's the signal!" the dark-haired woman says. (She's

(continue to the next page)

Beatrice, you think, and the blonde is Cornelia.) The creature disappears back into nothingness as quickly as it arrived.

"Interdimensional time goblins!" Chance exclaims. "How could you possibly be in league with those things? They're mindless abominations!"

"Indeed they are," Beatrice says. "As individuals. But gathered together in groups, they become quite chatty. Altogether *instructive*, as a matter of fact."

Chance strains against his captor's grasp, but even his impressive musculature is no match for iron limbs. Cornelia takes his square jaw in one hand and draws her face close to his.

"My sister and I have made a fortune trading with you time-hopping cretins, but every attempt to procure the power for ourselves has been thwarted by your high and mighty Time Patrol. The wee folk, however, have been much more willing to share resources."

"The goblins don't even *have* time travel technology," Chance says. "All they do is lurk between timelines!"

"You must learn to think *bigger*, my little patrolman. What these creatures are building is far beyond simple time-hopping. It's an infinite tapestry of tendrils reaching through every eon and every possible plane of existence. It's not simply traveling *through* time. It's complete control over the fabric of reality itself. And with our help, they've finished. All that's left is the one thing the wee folk can't provide themselves, which is a human intelligence to guide it."

"Or a pair of human intelligences," Beatrice adds, giddy.

You try to gasp, but with your mouth tied shut, all you achieve is a kind of muffled snort.

(continue to the next page)

"Horse!" Cornelia says. "Get the last of the equipment flown up to the arship."

The chief ruffian nods. "What about these two?"

"Take them outside and shoot them."

As the sisters storm off, Chance catches your eye again, giving you one of his cryptic nods. *What?* Last time that meant he wanted to go along with your captors, but he can't possibly be suggesting that you let yourself be *taken out and shot*, can he? If you ever get your jaw untied, the two of you are going to have a long conversation about nonverbal cues.

The thugs disperse, leaving just a handful to corral you and your partner. They loosen their grip and prod you toward the back door. If you were going to make a last-ditch, desperate attempt to escape your fate, this would be the time.

▶ *If you try to overpower the guards,* **turn to page 181.**

▶ *If you trust Chance's infuriatingly vague gesture and hold off,* **turn to page 134.**

Your choices here are "Tyrannosaurus rex," "dog," and "other." To be honest, we figured we could put blank pages at the end of the other two and no one would ever know. After all, the book isn't called *Time Travel Labrador*.

You inhabit the *heck* out of that T. rex. As your consciousness settles in, however, you find it to be a much bumpier ride than you anticipated. It might have something to do with how small your new brain is relative to your massive body or the fact that the dinosaur's physiology is so radically different from the mammals you're used to. Either way, this monster is *incredibly* difficult to control. It's a struggle just to keep its base instincts from taking over, much less focus on… um… whatever it was you came to the Cretaceous period for.

Betsy has scurried off while you've been getting your bearings, which is actually a bit of a shame, because now you really, *really* need something to eat. *So hungry*. SO VERY HUNGRY. Perhaps you'll be able to concentrate better once you get some food inside you?

▶ *If you go rustle up some lunch,* **turn to page 101.**

▶ *If you put all your energy into suppressing your hunger and overcoming your animal urges,* **turn to page 200.**

You're overcome with vertigo as your environs melt into a blur. *Again*? Now you're on the bridge of a spaceship, talking to a vaguely jellyfish-like creature that's hovering in mid-air. Your memories slowly catch up to your surroundings, and you remember that you're Twitch Richards, captain of the starship *Goldfish*. You completed a six-week certificate course in Space Captaining and everything. The floating jellyfish is Spot, your loyal second in command. He seems to be freaking out a little.

"Incoming transmission from Planet Patrol!" Spot says. "Earth is being attacked by evil overlord and racial stereotype Ted the Merciless!"

"Shields up!" you command. "Arm those laser torpedo things!"

"Um, about that," Spot says. "You're kind of being relieved of command. Planet Patrol isn't sure they can trust any officers of your... *ethnicity*. They gave the order that all ships must be commanded by persons of color, at least until we can determine the extent of the Caucasian Invasion."

"What? How are *you* a person of color? You're not even a *person*!"

"I'm a unique genetic creation," he says. "There's only one of me in the entire universe, which makes me as minority as they come. Plus, I'm Jewish."

Before you can protest further, he explains that he's not being made captain either. Your new boss will be X-9 the utility robot, who technically outranks you both.

The robot, it should also be noted, *loathes* you.

▶ *If you suck it up and take the demotion, doing whatever it takes to defeat the nefarious Ted,* **turn to page 138.**

▶ *If you straight-up mutiny,* **turn to page 157.**

If you're going to battle an evil lord, or whatever that guy is, you'd better get some practice in. You mess around with your new weapon until you can at least swing it around a bit without breaking one of your own ribs. It's quite a workout, and eventually you're so exhausted that not even the stench of your bedding or your mounting sense of dread can keep you from drifting to sleep.

You awaken the next morning covered with a coarse blanket, daylight streaming down from various holes in the roof above. Wait, wasn't your fight scheduled for dawn? Glancing around the room, you discover that your flail and shield are missing. Suddenly, you hear a cheer erupting from outside, coupled with a loud clang.

"Have at thee!" an unfamiliar voice yells. You wrap yourself up in your blanket—the proportions of your head and body are considerably different from the monkey folks in this reality, so it's not much of a disguise, but it's better than nothing—and peek out the front door. A crowd has gathered, obscuring your view, so you venture farther out for a better look.

"Move your giant head, crone," someone says from behind you. "I want to watch Lord Fenwick gut the vile creature!"

Sure enough, in a clearing ahead, you see the knight from yesterday doing battle with someone bearing your flail and shield, decked out in a full set of plate armor with a very large, demon-themed helmet, who nevertheless is most assuredly *not you*. Even more surprisingly, as you look on, the demon knight knocks Fenwick's sword out of his grasp and sends him clattering to the ground with one mighty blow.

"Free these good townsfolk from your oppressive rule, or

(continue to the next page)

suffer the consequences," the second knight says.

"I'd rather die," Fenwick sneers.

The victor pulls what appears to be a big, ornate pocket watch out from a chain under his breastplate, opens it, and sighs. "So be it," he says. There's a collective gasp from the crowd as he rains down one final blow, and Fenwick falls still.

He glances at his pocketwatch a second time. "Still?" he says. "Really? *Come on!*" He looks around, appraising the crowd. "Townsfolk!" he says, his voice booming. "Your oppressor is no more! You are free to lead lives of your own choosing, unencumbered by the shackles of tyranny!" He removes his helmet, revealing a face like a big, sunny Labrador.

That's not just a descriptive term. He literally has the head of a Labrador retriever. You certainly weren't expecting *that*. Did the people in this timeline evolve from both primates and canines?

"Demon!" someone yells. Apparently, they did not. "Dog demon! It's different from the one yesterday!"

"Kill the dog demon!" someone else shouts.

Whoever this Labrador man is, he fought in your place and definitely saved your life. You should probably step in and attempt to calm the townsfolk. Then again, the guy looks like he can take care of himself. Perhaps, you should take advantage of the diversion and just get yourself out of town?

▶ *If you try to convince the townsfolk to take things down a notch,* **turn to page 168.**

▶ *You know what? Screw these people. If you've had enough of the unwashed masses and sneak away,* **turn to page 242.**

You admire Velox's commitment, but you can hardly save the multiverse from interdimensional time goblins while dead.

"We need to leave immediately!"

Velox looks at you with chagrin and grave disappointment. "Fine," she says, moving toward a control console just in time to dodge a column of light erupting from above. "Everyone to the jump room!" she shouts into an intercom. "We'll put our faith in the Persistent Universe and go wherever and whenever it wills us."

"This *is* everyone," a small, terrified man says from across the room. "We're all that's left."

Velox's jaw tightens. "Time jump in three... two... one..."

The room fades to white and is quickly replaced by a very similar-looking room, only smaller and less filled with mysterious death rays and screaming. Apparently, the Persistent Universe agrees with Krikri, because you've been transported to the Temporal Custodians' remote training facility. You're also in the same exact moment that you left and not back in time, when you could actually do something about the goblin invasion. Which makes sense because, as far as you can tell, the Persistent Universe is as dumb as a box of rocks.

You try your time bracelet, but it's still inert. "That's the dampener field," Velox explains. "It prevents all unauthorized time travel, and from this facility, there's no way to shut it down."

"I may be able to help with that," Krikri says. "Or at least, I know some people who can."

With a soft pop, she disappears, much to the surprise of the Temporal Custodians. A blue portal opens up in the air where she was standing, and Krikri appears through it along with a

(continue to the next page)

muscular man in a leather jacket and… something that might be a sentient shrub wearing a lab coat. It rustles its foliage at you.

"My implanted technology is unaffected by the field," Krikri says. "And Professor Vegetatious here has jury-rigged some portal generators that are able to circumvent it as well."

You're impressed. "So now we go back in time and stop the goblin invasion before it starts, right?"

"No," Velox says. "The Persistent Universe wants us here, so this is where we fight."

"I agree," Krikri says. "The goblins exist outside causality. If they're making their move now, now is when we have to stop them."

"How, though?" you ask.

Krikri's naturally smiley dolphin mouth curls up a smidgen more. "With an army."

Suddenly, the room fills with portals, and time travelers of all descriptions begin stepping out of them. Part of you is tempted to dive into one at random before it closes and get out of this mess while the getting's good. Before you can seriously consider it, though, you feel Velox's hand on your shoulder.

"We're organizing into regiments," she says. "Come on. I've got just the detachment for you."

▶ Turn to page 222.

Somewhere in the multiverse there's a version of you crazy enough to take on a gun-toting madman while in the body of a Labrador retriever, but that version is not here. You back away slowly and break into a run just as the gun fires. One scientist howls in pain, another one yells in fury, and then the whole roomful starts wailing uncontrollably in some combination of shock, fear, and grief.

Alas, the merged clone, his mind made stronger by the combination of two alternate selves, did indeed have a vital role to play. Without him, the laser tower fires on schedule, and the shadowy creatures who set all of these events in motion to begin with are able to siphon off the discharged extradimensional energy to… well, it's a long story. But the end result is a catastrophic occurrence way off in 2271 that completely undoes the entire history of time in every possible universe.

Oh yeah, and the end result for you, personally, is being gunned down by a long-bearded scientist who has now gone completely over the edge as you try to sneak out the door. Let's hope the other, braver Betsy has better luck in her own timeline.

THE END

It takes the better part of two days to put together your posse, but you make sure everyone is armed with weapons that might be of use against a dinosaur (as opposed to some mythical creature). The local baron gets wind of your efforts and sends soldiers who operate giant crossbow contraptions that fire arrows the size of tree trunks. You send scouts to locate the monster's lair, and after sundown on the second day, you march upon it.

The beast sees your procession from its hilltop and tromps down to meet you. You recognize it instantly in the moonlight. "See, it's not a dragon at all," you say. "It's just a prehistoric Tyrannosaurus!" The dinosaur seems more interested in roaring and acting ferocious than actually biting anyone. The crossbow guys open fire, and your troops charge with their pitchforks and lances. The poor thing doesn't stand a chance.

You're a hero! The town throws a massive feast in your honor, which is great fun even though you stick to side dishes once you discover that the main course is an enormous, roasted dinosaur carcass. The townsfolk, however, can't get enough of it. Soon, rumors of the rare, delicious dragon have spread far and wide. Visiting noblemen stream into town, offering larger and larger purses for the last bits of dinosaur flesh. At which point, members of your troupe start looking at you funny.

What? Surely the bonds of friendship you've formed traveling with the Wondrous Freakporium outweigh any potential profit to be made by *selling you off as meat.*

Nope. Toby is wearing flame-repellent clothing and rubbed with deadly nightshade when he murders you in your sleep.

THE END

You have no idea how long you've been trapped in there, but you'll be damned if it's going to be one second longer. Well, one second longer than it absolutely has to be, at any rate—you still have to figure out how to get out since the doors aren't designed to open from the inside. The banging and crashing noises you make while trying to force them are accompanied by a similar cacophony from outside, and when you eventually rip the doors off their hinges, you find out why.

A gleaming, steel, mechanical version of yourself is feasting on the remains of the unfortunate saps you heard talking earlier. Your first reaction is to wonder why a robot dinosaur would even *need* to eat. Then it looks up at you and screeches, and you realize you have more pressing concerns.

Since your adrenaline is already pumping, you figure that a good offense is the best defense and lunge. The thing moves with

(continue to the next page)

terrifying grace, however, and dodges your attack with ease. You manage to connect with a tiny piece of its metal tail as it scoots past, but all you receive for your trouble is a broken tooth.

The robosaur coils, preparing to strike back. Uh oh. You're about ninety-five percent sure that a mouth full of polished steel teeth is the last thing you're ever going to see. Before it strikes, though, a glowing time portal opens up behind it. What? You don't feel gassy at all, so this can't be one of yours.

The mechanical monstrosity certainly weighs more than you do, but if you hit it just right, you might be able to knock it through the portal and into some other century. But then what? You'll still be trapped here in the Steampunk Basement of Broken Dreams.

▶ *If you try to get past your opponent and jump through the portal yourself,* **turn to page 23.**

▶ *If you settle for pushing Robosaurus rex into it,* **turn to page 118.**

Hey, remember when you chose the 1880s as your temporal destination because it seemed like it offered your greatest chance for survival? If someone else is volunteering as the turkey in this turkey shoot, far be it from you to get in her way.

If your marksmanship was as well developed as your self-preservation instinct, the plan might have worked, too. Alas, Cartwright bursts into the fray screaming and yelling and firing wildly while you take careful aim at one of the guards stationed in the rafters... and miss by a country mile. In fact, your first three or four shots are so off target that the snipers don't even realize they're being fired upon. It isn't until one of them drops Cartwright in her tracks that they notice that additional—if not terribly threatening—gunfire is coming from your position as well.

Then, they shoot you. Then, they shoot Annie and Bobbins. Then, they give each other high-fives, and then, their entire blimp explodes because the Powder Monkeys are really, really good at what they do.

Unlike *someone* we could mention.

THE END

If Beatrice was using the term "continental" at all literally, desperate measures are definitely in order. You throw yourself into the still-expanding plasma sphere and feel every cell in your body disintegrate completely upon impact.

Your consciousness, however, is absorbed into the orb. What you discover there is not so much *control* over the fabric of reality as a deep, cognitive *connection* to it—your awareness grows to encompass the entire breadth of creation in every single millisecond simultaneously throughout all time and an infinite spectrum of alternate realities.

It's kind of a lot to take in.

The first thing you realize is that the pending explosion is inevitable. Fortunately, it was never meant to happen in the skies above Chicago. You free the sphere of energy that's now the closest thing you have to a physical form from the airship and fling it at the speed of thought to the surface of the moon. Both because you want to save humanity from the blast and because the moon is simply where you will always live and always *have* lived. As the self-aware expression of the persistent universe, you'll find that the line between your decisions and immutable predestination is something of a blur.

You also realize that giving the universe the ability to make decisions was the interdimensional time goblins' plan all along. So that kind of worked out for them. But creation is better off with you in the cockpit than a pair of morally bankrupt 1880s crime lords, right? Or is the corrupting influence of consciousness itself all the goblins need to enact their nefarious plot?

It's a conundrum, but you've got all the time in the world to ponder it.

THE END

As painful as it is, you decide that your path and Krikri's are ultimately different ones. You insist on using the machine and tracking Von Krumpf on your own. So you set it for the morning in 1983 on which your journey first began. When you arrive, however, something is *horribly wrong*. You start to settle into the now very-familiar Betsy but are bounced out by another presence as if someone else was attempting to Bakulate into the dog at the same time you are.

You try again, using all your psychic strength to gain purchase in the animal's mind, and discover that the other consciousness is *you*. Of course it's you, transferring your consciousness in from Professor V.'s lab, just like you did when all this began. However, this is some monkey version of you from the alternate reality. It won't even *know* to change the universe back to the normal dinosaur timeline!

You feel your consciousness merging with your alternate self. Normally, two versions of the same consciousness would complement each other and create a stronger whole, but all the tachyon particles bouncing around the room from Von Krumpf's machine and your own repeated time jumps wreak havoc on the process. Your sense of self fades away as you're absorbed into the brain of monkey-you. It's incredibly disorienting.

Somewhere deep inside, however, you have buried memories of the dino-timeline, and your escapades with Krikri in 2271. With that advantage, you should be able to make AMAZING decisions from here on out.

Right?

▶ **Turn to page 1.**

Krikri is the only reason you've even survived this long in 2271, so if she needs your busted time machine, she's got it. You hand her the device, and with a soft pop, she's gone.

Forever.

Which is fine because you've decided to teach yourself spaceship repair and get your own damned self off of this desolate rock. You stick a bloody handprint on a volleyball-sized chunk of debris, name it "Spalding," and commit to the *Cast Away* thing full-on. It takes four grueling, lonely years, but you finally learn enough rocket science to be fully confident in the structural integrity of your cobbled-together goblin craft.

Unfortunately, Dunning-Kruger is in full effect, and you're suffering from a metacognitive inability to recognize your ineptitude *something fierce.* Your spaceship is terrible. Really, *truly,* the worst.

It explodes on liftoff, and in all the universe, only Spalding is there to mourn you.

THE END

Professor V. gives you a quick course in programming the time device—it's actually a lot like setting the clock in the dashboard of your car (which, to be honest, you've never successfully done). She sets it for the Temporal Activity Cluster in the Cretaceous period, trusting that, if you run into trouble, you'll be able to get yourself back. Of course, depending on how this mission goes, there may or may not be anything here to come back to.

You leap through the portal and find yourself hurtling through space and time. This trip seems to be taking much longer than the last one—makes sense, you think, considering you're traveling millions of years. The extended weightlessness is disconcerting, so you try to concentrate on the technicolor light show whirling around you. It's actually kind of relaxing.

That is, until a shadowy, gnarled little creature jumps onto your chest and claws you in the face.

Aaaaaaagh! Get it off! It twists and squirms and gets both its lumpy little hands on your time bracelet. Whatever it is, it's strong! You finally clamp down on its shoulder with your powerful dinosaur jaws (*super* gross tasting, just so you know) and manage to fling it away.

As you do, you hit solid ground with a thud. It knocks the wind out of you, but after a moment you regain your composure, pick yourself up off the ground, and look around. You're surrounded by poorly constructed thatch houses and a whole lot of mud. A mammalian creature dressed in what might be a burlap sack with a rope for a belt pokes its head around one of the buildings.

"Dragon!" he yells. "Or demon, or something!" What? That's rich, coming from a guy who looks like he evolved from a monkey, or possibly a lemur. You're pretty sure nothing should be speaking English in the Cretaceous period, however, so you check your bracelet and discover that the readout that should display the current date has gone dark. Uh oh. You try punching in the sequence to return you to Professor V.'s lab, but nothing happens.

That weird goblin thing that attacked you in the timestream *broke your freaking time machine.*

"Kill the dragon!" someone else screams. You see several additional monkey people approaching, carrying various types of crude landscaping tools. This is just a simple misunderstanding. You should be able to talk your way out of it, right?

▶ *If you explain to the growing mob that you're not a dragon,* **turn to page 226.**

▶ *If you assume the worst and run like hell,* **turn to page 80.**

As graves go, you'll take watery over disembowelly any day. You make it to the river's bank just ahead of the rampaging tyrannosaur and take the plunge, discovering immediately that prehistoric rivers are the *worst*. The rapids toss you around like a rag doll as you try desperately to dodge massive chunks of jagged rock and keep your head above water. This is some serious *Land of the Lost* business, and you don't even have the benefit of a tiny raft.

As expected, it culminates in a terrifying drop off a sheer cliff (since you pass out long before you reach the bottom, you're unable to attest to whether it plunges you fully a thousand feet below). You're halfway across Pangea by the time you regain consciousness on the banks of a much calmer tributary. You did it! Ha! Take *that*, tyrannosaur!

You locate a warm, hollow spot beneath the roots of a fallen tree and settle in for some much needed recuperation. That whitewater adventure messed you up pretty good. Also, your visit to the late Cretaceous has apparently coincided with the astronomical event that triggered the dinosaur extinction, because later that day all hell breaks loose. There's a massive explosion over the horizon, and subsequent earthquakes, volcanic eruptions, and blankets of ash further complicate your recovery.

Days turn into weeks as you slowly nurse yourself back to health amid the geological chaos. Progress is excruciatingly slow—even as you regain strength, odd things seem to be happening to your physiology. You find yourself getting tired easily, and your belly is increasingly sensitive, particularly around the…

(continue to the next page)

Nipples? Son of a bitch. Betsy's *pregnant.*

You were concerned about the history-changing impact of releasing a single dog into the prehistoric wilds, much less an entire litter! Still, what's the alternative? You've worked *incredibly* hard to keep Betsy alive, and the very idea of putting her children at risk is utterly abhorrent to you. Granted, that might be the canine pregnancy hormones talking.

When you decide to find somewhere else to park your consciousness and ponder your options, you're treated to another surprise. Whatever temporal mechanism usually connects you to your native time period is also responsible for your ability to jump hosts. The Labrador retriever's body is now yours, permanently.

Aw, crap. You're going to have to throw yourself off a friggin' cliff for the sake of the universe, aren't you?

▶ *If you make the ultimate sacrifice to prevent potentially catastrophic damage to the timeline,* **turn to page 126.**

▶ *If you chill the hell out and let the poor dog have her puppies,* **turn to page 209.**

Why mess around with outside observations when you can go right to the source? You settle into the mind of the mammalian scientist. What you find there, however, is utter madness. His thoughts are a jumbled mess of determination, loss, and rage, and you can't be certain if the images that flash by are memories or fragments from dreams. You can't make heads or tails of them. Suddenly, all the anger and animosity narrows to a focus and cuts through the haze of confusion like a knife.

He knows you're in there.

If you don't get out of this guy's head soon, it's absolutely going to drive you mad. You concentrate on breaking away and feel your awareness slip back to the laboratory in 2271. You quickly discover, however, that you're not alone. A piece of the scientist's mind *came with you.*

You can't be sure if it's truly a separate consciousness in your head or if you're just coping poorly with staring into the abyss of utter insanity, but either way, it isn't pretty. Krikri tries her best to calm you, but you're WAY past listening to reason.

Buckle in, because this is going to a dark place. What's a fun, conversational way to say that you're so desperate to silence the raging tempest in your head that you bash your own skull in with a 250-year-old chunk of scientific equipment?

Yikes. Apparently there isn't one.

THE END

You throw your lot in with Velox and her Persistent Universe (or, alternatively, just hesitate for the briefest moment since a second and a half is barely enough time to properly hurl yourself *anywhere*). With a flash of light, the interior of the moonbase is gone, and you find yourself in a familiar room. A thick-bearded, poorly groomed mammal-person with several pounds of machinery strapped to his chest is gesticulating wildly at a bored-looking Labrador retriever.

"THIS IS WHERE IT STARTS," a voice says inside your head. Oh no. *Not this again.* "VON KRUMPF GOES BACK IN TIME AND CREATES THEM! BUT HE ONLY CREATES THEM BECAUSE *THEY MAKE HIM GO BACK IN TIME!*"

"Creates who?" The Great Consciousness of the Universe, as usual, isn't making a ton of sense. Before you get your answer, though, the room dissipates and is replaced by open jungle. A huge metal tower sits in a clearing, surrounded by a horde of small, gnarled creatures. That dolphin lady Krikri and some mulleted guy are frantically trying to fight them off.

Also of note: a full-sized, prehistoric Tyrannosaurus rex appears to be battling a robot dinosaur.

"INTERDIMENSIONAL TIME GOBLINS!"

Once again, the scenery fades to white and is replaced by a modern street filled with ugly, angular cars and surrounded by a translucent dome.

"LOOK!"

The disembodied voice doesn't seem to understand that you can't see it *pointing*. A quick survey of the landscape, however, reveals thousands—possibly *millions*—of goblins piled on top of each other outside the dome.

(continue to the next page)

The things are super creepy. "What are they *doing* out there?"

"AMASSING! PLOTTING! *THINKING*. THEY'RE A HIVE MIND—INDIVIDUALLY THEY AREN'T TOO BRIGHT, BUT IF YOU CRAM THIS MANY TOGETHER, THEIR INTELLECT INCREASES EXPONENTIALLY!"

"You understand that you don't have to yell everything, right?" you say. "You're *literally* inside my head. I can hear you *just fine*."

The enthusiasm of the Persistent Universe, however, cannot be dampened. "THEY LIVE IN THE SPACE BETWEEN REALITIES! THOSE TIME PATROL GUYS BUILT THEIR HEADQUARTERS THERE AS WELL, AND THE GOBLINS FREAKIN' *SWARMED* IT. WITH SO MANY IN ONE PLACE, THEY HAD ENOUGH BRAINPOWER TO FORMULATE THEIR DASTARDLY PLAN!"

"*What* dastardly plan?"

The scene fades again, and this time you find yourself in what might be the interior of a huge sailing vessel. Ruffians and big, clockwork robots are scampering about in a blind panic.

"TO CREATE *ME*! TO GRAFT A LIVING INTELLI-GENCE ONTO THE FABRIC OF THE UNIVERSE! THEY WANT ME TO MAKE A CONSCIOUS DECISION THAT GENERATES A PARADOXICAL EVENT FOR THE *UNIVERSE* AND PEELS *ALL OF EXISTENCE OFF OF ITSELF*!"

Yikes. "Well, then *don't*."

"I WISH IT WERE THAT EASY," the voice says. A glowing sphere of energy mounted to the ship's ceiling flashes, and you find yourself back in Velox's moonbase.

(continue to the next page)

"THERE ARE FOUR CATASTROPHIC TEMPORAL EVENTS: 65 MILLION B.C., 1882, 2024, AND 2271. EACH EVENT CREATES ENOUGH STRESS IN THE TIMESTREAM TO ALLOW THE GOBLINS TO BREAK THROUGH!"

"Well, if these guys in 2271 are part of the problem, tell them to fix it! They worship you!" Great. It has you speaking in exclamation points as well. "They'll do anything you ask."

"NONE OF THEM CAN UNDERSTAND A WORD I SAY! *YOU* HAVE TO DO IT! THE GOBLINS CLOAK THEIR SHIPS BY CLOUDING THE MIND. IT WORKS ON THE CUSTODIANS SO WELL BECAUSE THEY'RE RELIGIOUS ZEALOTS—TRUST ME, YOU HAVE TO GET *PRETTY GOOD* AT IGNORING HARD FACTS TO CONVINCE YOURSELF THAT *I'M* A DEITY."

That does make sense. "YOU HAVE TO MAKE THEM BELIEVE IN INTERDIMENSIONAL TIME GOBLINS!" it continues. "CONVINCE THEM TO FIGHT!"

With that, the room flashes one final time, and the voice is gone. Velox rushes to you and grabs your shoulders. She looks distressed. "Where did the All-Knowing Consciousness take you? What did you see?"

Okay, this could be tricky. Velox clearly knows that *something* is making her people disappear. Should you level with her, be completely honest and hope she sees the logic of your argument? She's a grown monkey-person. She might listen to reason.

Alternatively, you could feed her a line of bull. That seemed to work pretty well before.

▶ *If you go with the truth,* **turn to page 257.**

▶ *If you make something up,* **turn to page 90.**

You can't bear the thought of Krikri buried alive beneath a goblin dogpile! To be honest, personal safety may have factored into your decision as well—you've seen your own throat torn out from up close enough times today, thank you very much.

Interdimensional time goblins, though, you can handle. By the time you reach it, the pile has grown to a sizable hill, but you tear goblins off with your teeth and hurl them across the landscape two and three at a time. Soon you've cleared away the entire clump, revealing...

An empty patch of ground.

Meanwhile, the robot reaches the tower and starts snapping girders off it like a popsicle stick sculpture. (Mad scientists, it turns out, are not famous for their architectural abilities.) The entire structure crumbles just as the laser is about to fire, causing a massive explosion that atomizes everything within the confines of the tachyon shield. You and your companions included.

Seriously, you've seen Krikri disappear into thin air at least twice in the last ten minutes alone. What on Earth made you think she needed *rescuing*? I'm not saying getting yourself eviscerated by a robot dinosaur instead would have made any huge difference, but *come on*.

Keep your head in the game.

THE END

You decide that, if you're going to create a time paradox severe enough to rip yourself free from the fabric of the universe, whatever that actually means, you'd better do the deed with your own tiny hands. You approach the bed, pulling the revolver that Professor V. gave you from the pocket of your ill-fitting dinosaur pants. You stare at your other self, resting peacefully.

Which is actually a bit of a miracle in itself, considering the unholy racket that timecycle makes.

Ready to do this?

▶ *If you pull the trigger,* **turn to page 147.**

▶ *Give me a minute, okay? Jesus! If you just want to make sure you've thought this through all the way before you do anything drastic,* **turn to page 228.**

The Cretaceous period is no place for delicate twenty-first century sensibilities! Your reptilian brain knows how to handle this threat, though. You let out a roar of your own and lunge, snapping your enormous jaws. The other creature may be bigger, but you give it the *crazy eyes*. After a minute or two of growling and snorting and making a fuss, it decides the picked-over edmontosaurus corpse isn't even worth it and backs away into the shrubbery.

ALL HAIL T. REX, UNDISPUTED MONARCH OF ALL DINOSAURS.

▶ **Turn to page 88.**

You've spent your entire life feeling like you didn't fit in. Your awkward childhood, all your years at school, your brief employment at the TTIA—you never quite *belonged*. And now you know why. It's because you belong *here*.

You tromp down the hillside to roar at the peasantry and demand tributes of gold. And possibly virgins. The peasantry, it turns out, are remarkably well organized. They carry long lances and pitchforks and, most notably, giant crossbow things that are loaded with sharpened tree trunks. Hmm. Those could be trouble.

You roar as fearsomely as you know how, but to your surprise, they don't scatter immediately. "See!" one of them shouts. "It's not a dragon at all! It's just a prehistoric Tyrannosaurus!"

What the…? You're almost positive that people in the Middle Ages didn't know anything about dinosaurs. You get a better look at their leader in the torchlight and discover that it isn't a person at all. More than anything, it looks like a miniature T. rex, only the size of a human being, speaking English and walking fully upright. How would something like that even *happen*?

You never find out. The mini-you barks an order, and suddenly you're inundated with sharpened logs and farm implements. You don't even get the chance to *mention* the hoards of gold because thanks to the dino-freak's clear-headedness, you're dead before your enormous body even hits the ground.

What an asshole.

The End

Krikri the Dolphin Lady offers you a replacement for your useless bracelet. "Remember, though, we need the power from the mothership cut off just as we approach the gateway," she says. "So don't shift unless you absolutely have to. Also, the ship is powered by a massive rift in space-time. The closer you get, the less likely this device will work at all."

Awesome. The custodians outfit you with laser pistols and space suits with jet packs mounted on the back. They also give you miniaturized nuclear devices that, if detonated inside the mothership's hull, should interrupt power to the shields moonside.

Six dino-soldiers seems like a pitiful attack force. "Don't worry," Veteran Time Patrol Dinosaur says. "Here's a trick I picked up during the Plutonian Chrono-Wars. If you survive this mission, just remember to travel back to this exact point in time and double up. Boom, twice as many T. rexes. Got it?"

You all nod in agreement. Then you sit in uncomfortable silence for a moment, waiting for reinforcements to show up.

They don't.

You suit up and launch into the void, thrusters blazing. As somber as the moment is, you have to admit that flying in a rocket-powered spacesuit is *pretty freakin' cool*. Soon, the mothership comes into view in orbit high above the moon's surface.

"There it is!" one of your companions says through your helmet's intercom. "Now, how do we—AAAAAAAAAAGH!"

A saucer-shaped craft roughly the size of a Winnebago appears out of nowhere, firing some kind of energy weapon into your formation. The six of you scatter as more UFOs materialize between you and your objective. There's another scream

(continue to the next page)

through your headset and a flash of light as one of your fellow soldiers goes down.

"I'm going in!" It's the low, rumbling voice of Giant Prehistoric Dinosaur. You see your comrade's massive form rocket toward the mothership, followed by a spectacular explosion that can only be the detonation of a nuclear device. You follow in the big tyrannosaur's wake and find a gaping hole in the mothership's hull. As you scoot through it, you hear two more soldiers fall.

"It's up to you!" Veteran Time Patrol Dinosaur says. "Pull the trigger! Pull the—"

The transmission cuts out. *Noooooooooo!* On instinct, you punch the button on your time bracelet, but the portal that appears before you is a sickly magenta color instead of the shimmering blue you were anticipating. It's also sort of flickering off and on. Krikri warned you that time travel might not work here. If you can't go back and try this whole invasion thing again, you really have no choice but to use your bomb. It isn't on a timer or anything, though, so that's a pretty grim option.

You notice that a huge, purple cloud dominates the ship's interior. Along with waves of energy, it seems to be radiating the sensation of *pure evil*. Hold on. The dolphin woman called that thing a "rift in space-time." It must lead somewhere, right?

▶ *If you fulfill your mission and blow yourself up,*
   turn to page 177.

▶ *If you take your chances with the sad little time portal,*
   turn to page 268.

▶ *If you toss yourself into the unspeakably evil goblin rift—because what could go wrong?—***turn to page 213.**

You're not about to hand over your only valuable possession—not to mention your actual HAND—to the first mysterious voice to ask for it nicely. Your mother didn't raise any fools.

Except, maybe she did? Before your cell door even opens, you realize that you've made a huge mistake. Through the bars, you see that this isn't the clockwork policeman at all. Instead, it's a large, ugly mammal-person with various pieces of machinery grafted to his body. One leg has been entirely replaced as well as both of his arms, and the result seems to have made bathing quite difficult because he looks like he hasn't had a shower in months. He flashes a terrifying, partially-toothed grin. You see that one mechanical hand grips the handle of a big, heavy revolver, and the other carries a rusty hacksaw.

If you're the type to be thankful for small favors, you'll be pleased to know that he uses the revolver first.

THE END

At least in the future you can't accidentally step on the wrong butterfly and wreck all of recorded history. Plus, they probably have cool rayguns and stuff. 2271, here you come.

Professor V. sets a return sequence on your armband, so you can get back in a hurry if something goes horribly wrong. Soon, you're hurtling weightlessly through a technicolor vortex and trying to keep your breakfast down. After a sudden jolt, the light show is replaced by sterile, white walls, and harsh lighting that doesn't seem to emanate from anywhere in particular.

Interestingly, you still seem to be floating.

You feel a jab at your backside, prodding you into a slow spin. The culprit is a woman in a silver jumpsuit who appears to be the same species of mammal as your mad scientist (although this one is completely hairless other than two well-manicured strips where her eyebrow ridges should be). She's wielding a plastic baton and a *severely* disapproving stare.

"Your presence in this timeline is unauthorized," she says. "No one travels to or from the 2270s without permission from the Temporal Custodians of the Persistent Universe." Something has gone horribly wrong! Frantic, you push the button on your time travel bracelet, but no shimmering portal appears.

"Only the Persistent Universe itself has power over the timestream here. Your primitive technology is useless."

Uh oh. "The persistent what, now?"

"The Persistent Universe is the all-knowing, self-aware expression of existence itself," she says breathlessly. "It's the force that compels paradoxes in the timestream to self-correct and flows through every corner of every reality in every era."

So your basic monotheism. "Gotcha," you say.

(continue to the next page)

Her lips curl up in a thin smile. "You needn't take my word on the matter," she says, tapping the wall with her baton. A circular doorway opens in the center of it. With another push, you begin to float down the hallway, now rotating end over end.

"Every traveler we pull from the timestream gets a personal audience," she continues. "The experience is wildly different for everyone but is guaranteed to change you forever. When confronted with the pure, timeless, omniscience of the Persistent Universe, most can't help but selflessly dedicate their lives to its service."

Okay, that sounds a little creepy. You float into a large chamber lined with floor-to ceiling pneumatic tubes big enough for a person to fit inside. "Of course, it has been known to reject applicants it finds unworthy," the jumpsuit woman says. "And occasionally…"

She gives you another tap with her baton, and you gently return to the floor, once again subject to the forces of gravity. "Occasionally, a lesser mind will consume itself attempting to come to terms with the sheer magnificence of it all," she continues. "The reward, however, is well worth any risk."

You see that most of the tubes have placards with labels like "Operations" or "Detention Level," but the sign on the opening in front of you simply reads "Up." Your captor holds out one arm, gesturing for you to step inside. Across the room, a tired-looking robot is loading plastic canisters into another tube with a sign that says "Waste."

▶ *If you attempt a daring escape into the garbage chute,* **turn to page 174.**

▶ *If you take your chances with the Self-Aware Expression of the Persistent Universe,* **turn to page 104.**

No one touches Krikri! The half of you that didn't just meet her is super protective of that dolphin lady. Besides, those guys don't look like the reasonable, let's-talk-things-over variety of raving lunatics to you. You grip the offending clone's coat with your teeth and fling him aside like a rag doll, then charge into the throng. Your goal is to scatter the crowd with a display of tyrannosaur ferocity, but you're fully prepared to back up your bark with some very literal bite if the things turn ugly. You're less prepared, however, for the high-pitched whine that comes from two of the scientists' chest rigs when they collide while fleeing from you in blind panic.

Components in a homemade time machine tend to be on the volatile side. And safety, in the mad science arena? Not job one. The resulting explosion is enough to knock your seven-ton frame off its feet, and the subsequent chain reaction causes hundreds of additional explosions that wipe every sign of the scientists and their camp right off the prehistoric map.

Krikri, at least, timeshifts to safety just before the blast. So that makes one of you.

THE END

Down it is. You leap into the tube and discover that it operates on some kind of futuristic technology rather than plain old suction. Soon, you're rushing through the inner workings of the base. The experience is quite comfortable.

Once you pop out the other side, it's less so. The first thing you see is a massive, pulsating machine that can only be the power core. The next thing you see is an entire buttload of interdimensional time goblins, apparently here to guard it. There's no time to waste. You hurl yourself into the generator.

Power core, meet authentic 1880s steampunk shock rod.

The resulting explosion is Michael Bay-level nutso. It completely incinerates the central part of the custodians' compound and reduces the rest of it to a crumbling pile of rubble. The goblins who aren't burned to a crisp are flung out onto the moonscape (and, due to the reduced gravity, in some cases land miles away).

In fact, if the creepy little things required oxygen, or atmosphere of any kind, Krikri's plan would have worked perfectly. Alas, this is not the case. The survivors regroup, multiply, and continue their nefarious scheme.

Only now you've blown up everyone with any hope of stopping them. Gold star for effort, though.

THE END

"Surely, we can find a way to get to that airship that *isn't* completely and utterly insane," you say. Chance looks dejected but agrees to play it your way, and the two of you set off to find alternate air transport. Soon, you stumble across a landing pad where steampunk cyborgs (or *steamborgs*, as you've decided to call them) are loading crates into a hot air balloon. Your partner quickly dispatches them, and soon, you're floating into the night sky.

Floating very, *very* slowly. Even after dumping the crates, it seems your craft wasn't designed for speed. "A missile would have been faster," Chance mumbles.

Faster to *what*? Certain doom? "I'm content with the scenic route, thanks," you say, glancing down at the gaslit streets… about ten feet below? Wow, that *is* slow. Suddenly, a shimmering portal opens beneath you, and a dolphin-headed woman pops out of it and checks something on her wrist. Then a pair of screeching goblin things emerge from the portal behind her and drag her back in, knocking her wrist device away in the process.

Okay, *that* was unexpected. You get a better look at the doohickey as it skitters to a halt beneath a streetlight. It's a *time travel bracelet*. If you've been having any second thoughts about joining the Time Patrol, it looks like fate may have just handed you a way out.

▶ If you're committed to seeing your mission through and stick with your partner, **turn to page 193.**

▶ If you bail on that guy and dive for the bracelet, **turn to page 243.**

You leap into the crack in the universe and IMMEDIATELY REGRET YOUR DECISION. It doesn't lead to some other place or time but to the *empty spaces between reality*. There's no earth beneath your feet or even any air to float through. There's only an infinite expanse of nothingness. Well, that and interdimensional time goblins.

The wretched, twisted little things sense your presence in their domain and swarm. You have no idea how they move through the void since you seem to be utterly helpless. In moments, you feel dozens of strong, wiry hands grabbing at you from every—OH GOD, THE CARNAGE! THEY'RE TEARING YOU LIMB FROM LIMB AND GOUGING OUT YOUR EYEBALLS, BUT YOU'RE STILL ALIVE AND CAN FEEL EVERY—AAAAAAAAAAAAAGH! WHY DIDN'T YOU CHOOSE THE DINOSAUR FEEDING FRENZY? WHYYYYYYYYYYYYYYYY...?

THE END

"Sir knight," you say, trying to sound more offended than terrified. "You would strike down an unarmed opponent?"

"Sure," he says. "Why not?"

That wasn't the response you were hoping for. Well, you're committed now. "I challenge you to a duel on the field of valor."

"Bah," he shoots back. "You're no knight and, thus, have no such privilege."

"But I am!" you insist.

"Oh? Who do you serve, then?"

Crud. "Um, Lord... *Balrog*?" you say, trying to come up with something vaguely evil-sounding. Maybe he'll be intimidated if he thinks you come from the pits of Hades or somewhere. "Duke of the seventh circle of... Mordor?"

"A demon knight," he says, stroking his ample chin. "Hmm. I've never vanquished one of *those* before. So be it. Fetch your sword and armor, and I'll give you a proper slaying."

"Right! It seems I've left them back in the, uh, cave," you say. "Wait here a moment, and I'll be back in a jiffy."

The knight frowns. "Smith! How quickly can you fit this demon knight with a fine suit of armor?"

A stumpy, thick-set man peers out from the crowd. "It's awfully funny-shaped, milord," he says. "A week, maybe?"

"Hmm. How about just a passable one?"

"Three days, milord."

"Well, see what you can come up with by morning. In the meantime, let's find accommodations for our guest." A pair of thuggish men in stiff leather—squires, perhaps?—emerge from the crowd and manhandle you into a nearby structure. The floor is loosely packed with filthy hay that smells mildly of excrement.

(continue to the next page)

You're not sure if this is a barn or if everybody in town lives this way. They shackle your leg to a beam that appears to be the only support for the roof overhead. After your captors leave, you poke at it cautiously, but it proves surprisingly sturdy. You spend some time tinkering with your time bracelet as well, but find it well and truly inert.

After an indeterminate length of time, the small child who you've decided is probably a girl enters the structure. She's dragging a small round shield and some kind of spiked ball and chain on the end of a stick. "Milord?" she says. "Or… milady? I'm sorry, I've never met a dragon demon monster before, so I don't know how I should address you."

Turnabout, you suppose, is fair play. "That's not important right now," you say. "Are those for me?"

"If you find them suitable," she says. "Papa is still working on your armor, but he'll have it finished in time for your slaying at first dawn. Would you prefer to wield this flail over the usual sword?" She glances at your stubby little arms. "I thought you might value the extra reach."

That's pretty thoughtful, actually. "What's your name?"

"I'm called Fleck," she says. No help on the gender front there. "Um, can I ask you a question?"

"Sure, knock yourself out."

"The land where you come from—is it nice? Or is it all fire and brimstone and boiling lakes and such?"

"Oh, it's nice, alright," you say with a sigh. "So comfortable and *clean*. I'm afraid I may never see it again, though. I appear to be stuck here."

"Oh, then you should visit the royal magician!" she says.

(continue to the next page)

"He appeared one day out of thin air, just like you. If anyone can get you home, he can!"

Royal magician? That sounds vaguely promising. "Say, Fleck. I don't suppose there's any way you could get me out of these shackles, could you?"

"Of course!" she says, pulling a ring of what appear to be identical iron keys from under her shirt. "Papa makes all the manacles in town as well. And you can hardly be expected to practice your dueling while chained up like that!"

You can't believe your luck! It'll be nightfall soon. Hopefully you'll be able to slip away under cover of darkness, and no one in this grubby little town will be the wiser.

Fleck finishes unshackling you and looks at you with big, brown, only marginally filth-encrusted eyes. "And I can trust you not to flee, of course?"

"Er," you say. "I, uh…"

"It's just that you're here under Papa's protection, so if you fail to appear on the field of valor, his life will most likely be forfeit," she says. "Mine too, I suppose."

Crap in a hat.

She leaves you alone with your thoughts, such as they are. You're not sure who came up with this code of so-called chivalry, but it pretty much sucks, you decide. Can you really abandon these innocent people to their probable death? Then again, you're no warrior, and are fairly sure that battling the knight will result in your *definite* death. It's not your fault that life for folks in the Middle Ages is flat-out awful, is it?

▶ *If you stay and face the knight in combat,*
  turn to page 36.

▶ *If you get the hell out of Dodge,* **turn to page 142.**

As much as you want to warn Krikri about the goblins' true intentions—whatever they even *are*—it's clear that there's no repairing the damage already done to your psyche. You tear yourself away from the time machine and take one for the team. Within minutes your mind is utterly gone.

By risking your own sanity to gain much-needed information and then ensuring that the cancer of madness couldn't spread to your alternate self, you've given your companions a fighting chance to stop the goblin horde. I know it doesn't feel like it, but you're a hero.

A crazy, crazy hero. It's not pretty, but still. Good work, my friend.

▶ *To find out what happened to the half of your brain that stayed in the Cretaceous,* **turn to page 217.**

"Stop!" you shout, emerging from the alley. The automaton and both children turn to face you, and you see that the kids are mammalian, much like the mad scientist was (though missing the face hair, which is an improvement). Monkey people! Are you too late? Should you have traveled further back?

The children immediately run away in blind terror—which makes sense, considering that from their perspective a talking dinosaur is probably FAR more terrifying than a robot policeman—and the automaton lurches toward you.

"Warning! All citizenry restricted to housing!" It quickly closes the gap between you—it's *much* faster than it looks—and hits you in the guts with its club, knocking the wind out of you. With a second blow, you fall like a sack of bricks on the cobblestone street.

"Warning!" there's a click as it switches pre-recorded messages. "Surrender or suffer the full force of law!" You look for a weak point in the thing's construction but are hammered with a third blow before you can get your bearings. This thing is pounding the *bejeezus* out of you. Your only hope is to surrender before it…

Wait a second. *You have a time machine.* Duh. You can be back home at the push of a button, sipping tea and *not* being pummeled by steam-powered robots. You haven't discovered much about the temporal anomalies of this century yet, though. Maybe you should just surrender and try to learn more? After all, your time travel wristband is pretty much the ultimate get-out-of-jail-free card.

▶ *If you get the hell out of the 1880s,* **turn to page 146.**

▶ *If you surrender, hoping to gather more information,* **turn to page 220.**

Yeah, that thing kills you. It had originally planned to just roar and stamp and make a stink until you backed off, which is how these disputes generally go. But when you made absolutely no effort to protect your soft underbelly, it figured what the hell. That dinosaur kills the *living crap* out of you. Then it proceeds to settle a dispute in the paleontological community about whether Tyrannosaurus rex was cannibalistic.

Turns out at least one of them was.

The End

You're not at all certain that you understand the ramifications of peeling yourself off the space-time continuum, but it seems like a big decision, and you'd rather not rush into anything. Besides, with the shield working, they'll be fine, right?

You enter the second portal and find yourself floating through the now-familiar light show. You brace for impact, hoping to keep your consciousness firmly embedded in your host—whatever era this portal leads to, you're pretty sure it can do without an uncontrolled, rampaging dinosaur.

When you pop out the other side, you're surprised to discover that it already has one.

The Tyrannosaurus that greets you in the cramped, blood-spattered laboratory is flat-out *pissed*. And apparently it takes the look of bewilderment on your face as a personal affront because before you can even begin to process what's happening, its teeth are at your throat. So your decision to avoid murdering one dinosaur essentially gets you killed by a different one.

Sorry. Time travel can suck that way.

THE END

You feel that you really sucked the marrow out of the whole interdimensional time goblin experience during the brief period you spent with one ATTACHED TO YOUR FACE. There's no way in *hell* you're going to just let them tractor beam you.

Krikri blips in and out of existence momentarily, which is unsettling until you find out why. "I just spent a couple of hours familiarizing myself with the ship's controls," she says. "Hold on to something." She engages in evasive maneuvers, but your little vessel is clearly outmatched. The craft takes heavy fire, knocking you off balance and sending you skidding across the floor.

"Just let them tractor beam us!" you say. "JUST LET THEM TRACTOR BEAM US!"

"It's too late. They've switched to weapons fire! We're getting close to the edge of the field—check your device!" Your armband's display lights have come back on, but hitting the "return" button still produces no results. Krikri rushes to your side.

"It looks like you've got temporal shift back but only enough power for a week or two at the most," she says. "And no location shift at all. How large of a portal can it generate?"

"No idea!" you say. "Why?"

"Because a week from now, this ship won't *be* here. If you travel in time but not space, you'll be floating in the void! We're going to need a portal big enough to drive the whole ship through."

She fiddles with the device for a moment, but another direct hit sends her scurrying back to the control station. "That'll have

(continue to the next page)

to do! I have no idea if this will work, but we're out of time. Set it for one week! Hurry!"

Professor V.'s instructions were complicated enough *without* the added pressure of a life-and-death space battle. "A week forward or a week back?"

"Doesn't matter!" The ship is rocked by another blast. "Pick one!"

▶ *If you set your armband to jump a week into the future,* **turn to page 208.**

▶ *If you set it for a week in the past,* **turn to page 153.**

You smack the scientist with your tail instead of going for the kill. When you think about it, all you really know about this guy is that he A) invented a time machine that breaks the fundamental laws of the universe, B) can rant with the best of them, and C) isn't a stickler for hygiene. Technically, you did see him murder someone in cold blood once, but that was a time-shifted alternate duplicate of himself, so maybe you can give him a pass?

The carnivore inside you is not pleased with your decision. Denied its meal, it lashes out in rage, and you're forced to battle the monster for control once again. As you deal with this distraction, the scientist stumbles to his feet and fiddles with his machinery, opening a time portal in the air in front of him.

(continue to the next page)

Before he can step through it, however, a figure emerges from the other side, blocking his escape. It appears to be a woman in a skin-tight space suit with the head of a... dolphin? The scientist takes one look at her and bolts in the opposite direction.

You're not sure if Dolphin Lady is friend or foe, but you suddenly feel a third presence inside your head. It doesn't feel like an aquatic mammal, though. If anything, you think it might be another dinosaur, only much smarter and significantly more relaxed than the one you're already sharing your body with. Could the dolphin be traveling with friends? Is there a dino-saur-headed space woman with psychic powers hiding behind a tree somewhere?

This new entity immediately starts trying to calm the tyrannosaur's rage and seems much better suited to the task than you are. You've found the T. rex increasingly difficult to control, so perhaps you should welcome this new influence. If it does manage to soothe the savage beast, though, what then? Can it control you as well? Maybe you should be helping the dinosaur defeat the floating consciousness instead.

▶ *If you team up with the new consciousness against the Tyrannosaurus,* **turn to page 254.**

▶ *If you team up with the Tyrannosaurus and try to force the new presence out of your mind,* **turn to page 130.**

You're not sure what time this is, but when monkey people start yelling things like "dragon" and brandishing farm equipment, it's definitely time to go. You run as fast as your powerful dinosaur legs can carry you, which is actually pretty fast. Before long you've left the angry townspeople far behind.

Now the sun is going down, and the air grows chilly. You keep traveling, hoping to stumble upon something you can eat or disguise yourself with, but have no luck. The only thing anybody seems to farm around here is dirt, and the clothesline conveniently hung with cozy blankets that you pictured in your head never materializes. Hours into the evening, your exhaustion finally grows stronger than your hunger or your chill, and you find a secluded spot under some brush away from the road and fall asleep.

It's not quite secluded enough. The following morning, you're awakened by something poking you in the stomach.

"'Tis alive!" someone says, prodding you again. "Ooh, and right hideous, too."

"Quit it!" you mutter, still mostly asleep. You vaguely remember your older sister waking you up by poking you with things when you were young. "Mom! Vanessa's poking me!"

You finally pry open your eyes and see two men in robes looking down at you. They look nothing like your sister Vanessa. The larger one has a big, heavy stick in one hand, which explains the poking.

"And it speaks!" the big one says. The smaller man stretches up on his toes and whispers something in his companion's ear. The big man's eyes widen. He smiles, drops his stick, and reaches underneath his robe for something. If he's going for a weapon, you're in trouble. You try to scramble to your feet but slip on the scattered leaves you had been using as a bed. You fall squarely on your tail, utterly at the mercy of the robed duo.

Fortunately, what emerges from beneath the cloak is a piece of parchment and a quill pen.

"Crabbe and Toby, of Crabbe and Toby's Wondrous Freakporium," he says proudly, "at your service." Surprised, you grunt a hello back at him.

"Toby believes folk will pay handsomely to see a speaking dragon," the big man says. The little one just nods. "So what say ye? 'Tis a standard contract."

What are the chances that these two lure you back their camp and murder you? Crabbe notes your hesitation. "Ah, but you needn't decide in haste," he says. "Come meet the rest of the company! We've got breakfast going!"

Your gut rumbles loudly at the mention of food—you're not used to going this long between meals. Perhaps the potential rewards justify the risk?

▶ *If you're swayed by the proposition of breakfast and follow them,* **turn to page 127.**

▶ *If you turn down their offer—their delicious, delicious offer—***turn to page 291.**

Yeah, you're pretty sure that river is going to kill you. You veer away from it and haul ass until the dinosaur is right on your heels, about to pounce. Then you dig your paws into the turf, dart directly between its legs, and scamper off into the underbrush. Your pursuer reels back in surprise and loses its footing, tumbling thirty feet across the forest floor and rooting up several saplings before skidding to a halt.

Holy crap—you should seriously consider being a Labrador full time because your ninja acrobat dog moves are *spectacular*. You push through the foliage until you're certain you've ditched the carnivore, then use your keen canine senses to locate the scientist. The Cretaceous period is full of radically new sights and smells, but fortunately, his aroma is both distinctive and powerful. You follow his scent to a wide, empty clearing where you find him gesticulating wildly, trying to explain something to...

Another identical mad scientist? Uh oh. You hide behind something vaguely fern-like and watch as three more duplicates pop out of shimmering portals. Suddenly, you realize that the clearing isn't empty at all, but filled with a wide assortment of tents and makeshift shelters. A crew of doppelgangers is looking over blueprints and clearing crates from the center of the encampment, and as they finish, an enormous steel tower of dubious construction appears on the spot. "Appears" may be the wrong word, though, because of course it was already there. *It's always been there.*

Wow, that escalated quickly. As you survey the bustling village of scientist clones, you hear rustling leaves and an all-too-familiar voice behind you.

"I did it, Betsy! Ah ha ha ha!" It's one of the scientists, wild-eyed and frothy-mouthed as ever. "Is it really you? Are you here in the flesh? But of course you are! A floating spy means an empty Betsy can't be far behind!"

His ranting draws the attention of several others, and soon you're surrounded. "Here, Betsy!" one of them says, dropping to his knees and patting the ground in front of him. "Good girl, Betsy!"

"Yes!" another exclaims. "You must come see the tower, Betsy. Everything *makes so much sense* inside the tower." A third scientist is just staring at you, gritting his teeth and shaking.

"Get the dog in the tower," he mutters to himself under his breath. "Get the dog in the tower... Get the dog in the tower..."

Okay, this is creepy as balls. If you hope to find any clues to what these madmen are up to, though, you know where to look. Granted, from the way they're acting, they seem as likely to cook you and eat you in there as give you the grand tour. Should you risk it?

▶ *If you enter the misshapen tower with the legion of crazy people,* **turn to page 244.**

▶ *If you turn tail and flee while you still have the chance,* **turn to page 152.**

"Yup, totally peeled off," you say. "I murdered myself *so* hard."

"Good!" the officer says, grabbing you and pulling you onto the seat behind him. Before you know it, the motorcycle lurches forward, and the room around you is replaced by a flash of swirling color. A few seconds later, you screech to a halt in the middle of a busy street. The moment you do, a siren starts wailing, and people all around you panic, running in every direction.

"Wow, Time Patrol HQ is intense," you say.

"This shouldn't be happening!" Bruxelles says. "The shield has failed! But this is impossible! Unless…"

A small mammal-woman in a lab coat runs toward you. "Mr. Bruxelles!" she says. "Someone here isn't peeled off of space-time! The delicate tachyon balance that sustains our shielding has been ruptured! Evacuate the base before it's too late!"

The motorcycle lurches forward and sends you toppling right off the back. You pick yourself up and dust off. The woman in the lab coat is staring at you. "Wait a moment," she says. "Who are you?"

Before you can explain yourself you hear a little popping noise and see a second woman—this one with the head of a dolphin and wearing in a skin-tight space suit—materialize out of thin air.

"Professor V.!" she says. "I see you're a mammal in this timeline. Do you happen to be an expert on tachyon shielding as well?"

Hey. This little gray-haired monkey person can't possibly

be Professor Velociraptor, can she?

"As a matter of fact, I am," the lab coat woman says. "And *you* would be…"

"I'll explain when we get there," the dolphin says. She grabs the professor's arm, glances your way, and waves. "Oh! There you are. See you in the Cretaceous!"

The dolphin woman pushes a button on her armband—it looks a lot like yours but quite a bit more weathered—and jumps through a time portal with the lab coat woman. Alas, it closes almost immediately, before you have the chance to follow. You figure they have the right idea, though—whatever's going on here, you're probably better off elsewhere, regardless of the nebulous Temporal Custodian threat.

Just as you turn your attention to your own time bracelet, something small and vicious attacks you in the face. Blinded, you feel a dozen more hands grabbing you at once.

"Interdimensional time goblins!" someone yells. "Ruuuuuuuuuuun!"

You don't know what an interdimensional time goblin is, other than "something nasty that attacks in waves, piling on their victims and ripping them limb from limb."

You never find out.

The End

If there's any chance these people are going to let you just mosey out of their villainous lair, you're not about to pass it up. Shockingly, they actually do let you go. You make your way back to the Gas Can hideout and, from what you can tell, aren't even followed (although you suppose you can't rule out invisible steam-powered spy drones—the technology in this timeline is monumentally screwy).

Annie is delighted to discover that her ridiculous hat device has gathered all the data she needs. "It's a good thing we sent you, too," she says. "Some of the stuff they've got tucked away is far beyond what we imagined."

"So now we attack!" Cartwright says. She's got various maps and plans spread out over a table and looks as though she's been champing at the bit all afternoon. Although you hate to rain on her parade, you continue your debriefing and tell them about your conversation with Beatrice. According to her, the compound isn't even the sisters' true base of operations. All the good stuff is in the secret airship.

Cartwright's jaw quivers. "But we have *all these plans* to attack the compound," she says. "Once we take it, we'll control their clockwork army and can worry about the rest afterward. Besides, how would we even *get* to their airship?"

Annie flashes a huge smile and jumps out of her seat, darting away into another chamber.

"No, no, no," Cartwright says, shaking her head. "There's absolutely no way you're getting me into one of those godforsaken contraptions."

"But they're perfect!" Annie shouts from the other room. "With our new power source, they'll be airworthy for certain!

I'm sure of it!" She pushes a bizarre machine into the room that looks like a bicycle with one wheel much larger than the other strapped to a pair of mechanical wings. "Ladies and gentlemen," she says through an ear-to-ear grin, "I present to you…"

She stands aside and stretches both of her arms toward the monstrosity with a grand flourish. "The ornithoptivelocipede!"

▶ *If you like the idea of attacking an armored blimp in the bastard love child of a failed attempt at a bicycle and a failed attempt at a helicopter,* **turn to page 231.**

▶ *If you agree with Cartwright and would rather keep the fight on solid ground,* **turn to page 110.**

Fig. 1. Ornithoptivelocipede

If there was ever a reason to maintain human consciousness while inside the body of a 7-ton killing machine, you sure can't remember what it was. You drop the pretense and go full T. rex. And it's awesome! Nothing messes with a T. rex! The only things you have to worry about are potential nosebleeds from HOW HIGH UP THE FOOD CHAIN YOU ARE.

You spend the next couple of hours tromping around, roaring with abandon, eating what you please, and making certain other area carnivores know you're not to be trifled with. All said, it's a pretty sweet gig—at least until mid-afternoon, when a stray comet hits the earth and causes a global extinction event. Crap on a Twinkie! You *completely forgot* about the global extinction event. The resulting change in climate and atmospheric conditions will fully eradicate your species from the planet within a few thousand years.

Since the giant space rock literally crushes you beneath it, though, it completely eradicates your sorry ass significantly faster.

THE END

BUT YOU ALREADY KNOW WHAT'S GOING TO HAPPEN.

Your doppelganger sees you coming and lunges at you, grabbing your gun arm and grappling you in a weird kind of dinosaur bear hug. And this time when the gun goes off, the blood you get spattered with isn't "yours" as in "I have blood exactly like that," but "yours" as in "the stuff that is supposed to be pumping vital oxygen to my brain."

Then the other you goes on to repeat your mistake, again and again, ad infinitum. It's like the shortest, goriest, weirdest *Groundhog Day* remake ever.

THE END

You've waded through enough internet comment sections to know that logic is the *worst* way to win an argument. "Our enemies have found a way to use our very strength—our unshakable faith—against us!" you say.

Velox gasps. You explain that you were able to see the attacking ships only because your devotion to the Great Consciousness is flawed—your enemies can hide in the imperfections of lesser minds, so only the unworthy can see them. It's not *terribly* far from the truth.

"Damn me and my perfect, unshakable fortitude!" she says. "How do we fight what we can't even *see*?" Around you, miscellaneous custodians are still disappearing into columns of red light. Suddenly, the floor shakes beneath your feet.

A familiar, melodious voice cuts through the din. "We have to evacuate. They're tearing the base apart."

"Agent Krikri!" Velox says. "You've returned! Have you been afflicted with the crisis of faith as well?"

Krikri looks at you quizzically, and you nod. "Um, sure," she says. "We need to get the crew to safety—is there somewhere we can retreat to?"

"There's a training facility on the dark side of the moon," Velox says. "But the gateway to the Great Consciousness is here—we can't abandon it!"

"We've already lost this battle," Krikri says. "We need to regroup to have any hope of winning the war."

Velox doesn't budge. "The Great Consciousness *is* the war. If we lose it, we lose *everything*."

▶ *If you agree with Velox and stand your ground,* **turn to page 235.**

▶ *If you get the hell off that base,* **turn to page 38.**

"What the hell," you say. "I'm in."

"Then come help me with these bloody things!" Bruxelles shouts. Oh, yeah. You sort of forgot about that guy.

You charge out of the tower and scoop half a dozen inter-dimensional time goblins into your gaping maw. Truth be told, hunger pangs may have played a significant role in your decision to stay. You chomp down and are shocked to discover that the little bastards are *delicious*. Seriously, they taste like *popcorn*. You immediately snatch up another mouthful.

Bruxelles has somehow managed to lose his shirt and jacket—his smooth, hairless musculature glistens with sweat as he pummels goblins with some style of martial arts that relies heavily on backflips and dramatic leg splits. His motorcycle time machine, alas, lies across the landscape in pieces, so there will be no help from that quarter.

Krikri joins you as well, wielding a long stick with a stone affixed to the end that seems to completely delete her targets from existence upon touch. You quickly clear the immediate vicinity, but the cracks in the sky remain open, and now goblins drop through by the *thousands*. You'll be crushed under an ocean of popcorn if something doesn't change quickly.

Quickly? "Wait!" you say. "We have freaking time machines! Why don't we just go back and do all this yesterday?"

"The tower wasn't ready yesterday," Krikri says. "And anyway, it ties into the positions of planets in orbit." She checks her watch. "If it's going to fire, it's going to fire in about six minutes. We have to figure out a way to keep the goblins away until then."

"At headquarters, we have a tachyon shield that keeps them

(continue to the next page)

out," Bruxelles says. "If only Professor V. was here."

"Professor V? As in Venkataraman?" You know her!

"Sometimes she's called that, yes. It's complicated."

"If I fetch this professor," Krikri says, "could she help us construct something of a similar nature here?"

"Maybe," Bruxelles says with a shrug. "Without a timecycle, though, you can't get through the shield to ask her. It keeps out unauthorized time travelers, too."

"I'll find a way!" With a pop, Krikri is gone. Sure enough, a time portal immediately opens, and she emerges from it with your boss in tow. The professor looks much as you remember her, but her hair is streaked with gray, and the lines on her face have deepened.

"Looking good, Professor V!" Bruxelles says. "No time to chat, though. Goblin attack! How fast can you throw a shield together?"

"Speed is irrelevant," she says, pressing buttons on a silver armband. Another portal opens behind her. "I'll do it last week."

The moment she steps through, a huge, shimmering dome appears around the camp. It pulses for a second, then dissipates in a burst of static. The professor comes running from the tower. "It's not working!" she says. "Is everyone here peeled off the space-time continuum?"

"I am!" Bruxelles says.

"Me too!" Krikri agrees.

"I am as well!" Hercule shouts from inside.

Oh, no. You vaguely remember that your dinosaur self might have been peeled off of space-time, but most of the memories from that universe are gone. "I'm not a hundred

(continue to the next page)

percent sure what that means!" you say.

Professor V. quickly explains that in order to peel yourself off of the space-time continuum, you need to create an extreme paradox by going back in time and killing yourself, just as Von Krumpf did when you first met him. She fiddles with her armband, opening a portal, and gestures at you to enter.

"But... kill myself?" you stutter. "I'm not sure if I can..."

She frowns, and a second portal opens alongside the first. "This one will take you safely away, then. Unless you're peeled off, the shield can't function with you inside." This professor seems significantly less patient than the one you ate breakfast with before work this morning.

"You don't have to go back in time and murder yourself," she says, "but you can't stay here."

> ▶ *If you choose the first portal and complete the gruesome task so you can stay and help defend the tower,*
> **turn to page 182.**

> ▶ *If you think they have it covered, take door number two and skip the self-assassination business,*
> **turn to page 75.**

You wrench the glowing armband from your double's wrist and disentangle yourself. Then, you smash it to bits with the butt of your revolver, surprised at how easily it shatters. Time travel bracelets: not super rugged, it turns out.

The shimmering portal immediately blinks out of existence. Unfortunately, you may have to work a little harder if you want to keep the timeline paradoxical—your alternate self is eyeballing the bracelet on your own arm with an unsettling, lustful look. Viewing yourself from across the room is always going to be weird, but this facial expression is making the experience particularly off-putting.

"Just let me see it for a second," your double says. "I won't push any buttons or anything, I swear." Wow. You never realized what a *horrible* liar you were.

"You see?" Professor Velociraptor says. "As long as there's any ambiguity at all, the timestream will try to correct itself. Even if you destroy both time bracelets—and *please do not do that*, they cost six billion dollars to manufacture—the universe will find some way to circumvent paradox. Where there's life, there's—"

She's cut off by a loud screech and a flash of light, and suddenly you're confronted by a rugged-looking man in a leather jacket dismounting a futuristic motorcycle right in the middle of the lab. Like the mad scientist, he's weirdly mammalian, as if he had evolved from some species of ape.

"I've got a report of an unauthorized time-shifted duplicate," he says in an accent that's vaguely European but hard to place. "Time license and time registration, please."

He's square-jawed and muscular, and even as a dinosaur,

(continue to the next page)

you think his short-in-front, long-in-back haircut looks goofy as hell. He also seems to place emphasis on unusual syllables, making his speech that much more difficult to parse. "Professor V.," he says. "Looking good! How long have you been a lizard monster?"

This catches her off guard. "Do I know you?"

"It's me, Chance Bruxelles! But you might not have met me in this reality. I can never figure out how this time travel stuff is supposed to work."

As they chat, you see your doppelganger slowly edging toward the officer's still-running motorcycle. Uh oh. If you felt powerfully compelled to correct a paradox, you'd probably try to steal a time machine, so it's a safe bet your other self is thinking the same thing. You glance at the enormous sidearm strapped to the officer's belt. This can't be a good idea.

Or can it? If your doppelganger is shot and killed by someone other than you, does that still count as a paradox, and peel you off of space-time? You feel bad for considering it, but that other you is kind of a pain in the ass, and it might actually solve your problems if you just let this scenario play itself out. Or would the past ten minutes of your life just re-write themselves without you in them? Is that a risk you can afford to take?

Your double jumps onto the motorcycle with a squeal of glee.

▶ *If you try to tackle you before you manage to get you killed,* **turn to page 210.**

▶ *What? Even the GRAMMAR of that option is too complicated to deal with. If you just let the damn fool go,* **turn to page 139.**

You've been trying to stop this guy from catastrophically altering the timeline, and now the time police show up to arrest him? Sounds like a win-win. Besides, you're pretty sure watching the cop try to corral several hundred raving lunatics is going to be entertaining as hell.

On that last point, at least, you aren't wrong. New scientists pop out of time portals faster than Bruxelles can apprehend them, and soon, his own multiples are racing in on timecycles to join the fray. Their numbers grow exponentially like a timeshifted-alternate-self arms race, and you can almost hear the *Benny Hill* music as they chase each other around the campsite. The landscape is so packed with doppelgangers that the mysterious interdimensional figures pulling Von Krumpf's strings from behind the scenes can't even move forward with their nefarious plot. They give the whole thing up as a lost cause and move on to plan B.

The comet that they've chucked toward the Earth is still on its way, though. And you're still engrossed in the hijinks when it comes rocketing through the cloud cover and crushes you beneath it like a bug.

THE END

Since you'd like to avoid the inevitable heat death of the universe (or whatever it is that keeps agents from returning from 2271) and everyone knows prehistoric eras are just a recipe for time travel disaster, you play it safe. This time, when you find yourself in the alleyway in 1882, you see the backside of your previous self rushing off to help the children. You start to follow—let's see how that police robot fares against TWO helpless tyrannosaurs!—but are cut off abruptly by a futuristic motorcycle that screeches out of nowhere and narrowly avoids crashing into you.

The thing has two riders, and one of them hops off the back of the bike and rushes toward you, sweeping you up in a big bear hug. "My friend! I was afraid you had perished aboard the airship!" He's mammalian, his accent is vaguely European, and his haircut is all-business up front and party in the back. You've never seen him before in your life.

"Um, do I know you?"

"It's me, Chance Bruxelles! I helped you murder yourself in your sleep, to peel yourself off the space-time continuum!"

You're actually pretty sure Professor V. helped you with that. "No matter," he continues, "the important thing is that you're alive! Now, have you seen my motorcycle around here anywhere?"

"Uh, isn't *that* your motorcycle?" His monkey-person companion gives a little wave and then revs up her motor and disappears into the timestream.

"No, Officer Kowalski just gave me a ride back, so I could tie up some loose ends. Come on, you can help me search! I seem to remember you were there when we rescued ourselves from the

(continue to the next page)

Steampunk Mafia, so it's probably best if we team up anyway."

Okay, none of that made any sense to you. Chance explains that he's an officer of the Time Patrol, an agency from further in the future than your Time Travel Investigation Agency, which sounds about forty times cooler. You spend a few hours wandering the city with him, half-heartedly looking for his time machine. Apparently, it's shielded against the type of scanners his organization uses to find out-of-place technology, which keeps it hidden from other time travelers but is kind of a double-edged sword if you forget where you parked.

You try to grill him on the mechanics of time travel, but he's frustratingly vague. He keeps talking about the significance of choosing between two different cookies, but he doesn't actually have any cookies (which is a shame because darkness has fallen, and all this walking around alternate 1880s steampunk Chicago has made you hungry).

"Which reminds me!" Chance says. "When you meet your other self, do not say anything about your future! Just let what's going to happen happen. If you start giving yourself doubts, you'll wind up screwing everything up."

You round a corner and catch a glimpse of another version of Chance and another version of you being taken prisoner by a band of steampunk-looking cyborgs. "Aha, it's time!" Chance says. "Hurry around back, so we can thwart them when they take us out to be shot!"

You follow him around the building and wait next to a huge, copper missile thing that's just leaning, unguarded, against the wall. Chance mentions something about planning to ride the

(continue to the next page)

missile up to some villain's secret airship.

It sounds like a *terrible* idea. "We're going to ride *that thing*?" you ask.

"No," he says, "we already did! To the airship? Remember?"

"That wasn't me! Wait..." you recall something he said earlier. "I don't *die* up there, do I?"

Before he can answer, a door opens, and your companion bursts into action, knocking out four armed guards with a whirlwind of punches and kicks. You have to admit, it's impressive as hell. Soon, you stand face-to-face with your identical duplicate. Chance quickly unties his own double and spends a minute engaging in chest bumps and high-fives with him while you struggle with your counterpart's ropes.

"So," your doppelganger asks once you've finished, "you're *me*? From the future?"

Chance told you not to get into specifics. But there's something screwy about the order of events he's presenting. Should you at least warn yourself that you're not some kind of future proof that whatever scheme these guys are hatching is going to turn out well?

▶ *If you tell your double you have no recollection of any of this,* **turn to page 267.**

▶ *If you just smile and nod,* **turn to page 164.**

You decide to try the diplomatic approach. If nothing else, maybe you can hide in a storage compartment or something and sneak out later. It beats getting shot out of the sky, right?

Alas, interdimensional time goblins don't need much in the way of storage space. You're still scrambling for a hiding place when your craft's dome splits open to reveal dozens of chittering goblin faces peering in at you. The mothership looks to be one big chamber with a massive, purple energy cloud filling the bulk of it. The walls are covered in jagged handholds with goblins scurrying across them at great speed.

Did we say dozens? Closer inspection reveals *thousands* of them.

Krikri's narrow little dolphin jaw drops. "I'll try to bring help," she says, handing you her egg stick. Suddenly, with a soft pop, she's gone.

Goblins approach from all sides, and they don't look like diplomats. You note that some of them are emerging from the purple cloud—could it be some kind of a portal to somewhere? There's a fairly clear path to it, but just the idea of entering the thing fills you with dread. It's as if it were filled with so much evil—like, *ancient, unspeakable* evil—that it couldn't contain it all, and some was leaking out.

What else can you do? Sit tight and see if they take you to parlay with their Goblin King? With a Hobbit-style scrotum beard? You cringe at the very idea.

And that's the *best case* scenario.

▶ *If you make a run for the terrifying cloud that almost definitely leads to certain doom,* **turn to page 213.**

▶ *If you stay and talk it out,* **turn to page 129.**

A quick whiff with your humongous new nasal passages reveals a large group of edmontosaurs nearby, so you lumber toward them at top speed. On average, those things are actually quite a bit faster than you, but in a pack that size, there are usually at least a couple of...

Bingo. The herbivores bolt as you burst out of the treeline, but one of the older specimens twists a leg on a fallen branch and hits the ground with a thud. You descend upon that poor duck-billed son of a bitch and rip out its throat before it even knows what hit it. Then you proceed to devour its soft, fleshy bits with abandon.

You had hoped that satiating your hunger would quiet the roaring tyrannosaur inside you, but alas, the opposite is true. With the savage display of carnage, your animal instincts take over and threaten to drown out the last vestiges of your evolved consciousness completely.

▶ *If you fight with all your might to retain some shred of humanity,* **turn to page 170.**

▶ *If you just go with it,* **turn to page 88.**

Knowing is half the battle, right? You peel yourself off the floor as quietly as possible and press your dinosaur earhole against the wall. At first it's just the two voices, who seem to be exploring the basement workshop for the first time, trading quips back and forth.

Then the screaming begins.

You hear an unsettling clang of metal scraping against metal, accompanied by a high-pitched mechanical screeching and the terrified cries of two people being eviscerated by something huge and possibly robotic. Holy *crap*. You're feeling better and better about your decision to play this one safe.

After a moment (whoever those two were, at least their demise was swift), the room falls quiet. Hmm. How long should you wait after listening to a nightmarish giant robot massacre before poking your head out to see if the coast is clear? Just as you decide to risk a peek, you hear someone bound into the room, cackling like a madman. The first thing he does is throw the switch to your stasis chamber, and you immediately shift into time dilation again.

Son of a *nutcracker!* Whatever your potential window of escape was, you've missed it. How long will you have to wait in timeless slumber before someone finally revives you again?

Fortunately, all of North America explodes a few hours later, so you never have to find out.

THE END

If you can't trust ranting, bearded lunatics with giant laser cannons, who can you trust? You take your chances and go limp as the doppelganger heaves you unceremoniously into the pulsating blue beam. Your physical body is instantly atomized, but your consciousness shoots out into the multiverse, rocketing millions of years into the future and sideways through alternate realities until you finally settle in. You open your eyes slowly and find yourself inside what appears to be a giant cardboard box amidst a rambunctious pile of Labrador pups.

This isn't your ideal timeline at all. It's *Betsy's*.

A heartbreakingly adorable little girl sporting unruly afro puffs grabs at the puppy next to you. "This one!" she says, but it squirms out of her grasp before she can separate it from its littermates. Undeterred, she snatches you up instead. "No, this one!"

On the way to the counter for shots and paperwork, you pass a forty-something, beardless Science Man, looking for all the world like he's one canine companion away from utter despair. Wait! If you go with him, you'll be there when he opens the time portal a few years from now, and you can try again! However, the merged consciousness of adult and puppy Betsy is in control. And it's already licking the little girl's face like she's made of candy. Like it or not, you're trapped here in a life of belly rubs, Milk-Bones, and long afternoons chasing tennis balls around the park.

When you stop to think about it, that actually sounds *amazing*.

THE END

It's a tough call, but you decide that "the all-knowing, self-aware expression of existence itself" probably offers better odds than "waste." You suppose that a third option might be to try overpowering the woman in the jumpsuit, but she clearly isn't messing around with that plastic baton. You step inside the tube marked "up."

Just as advertised, you slowly begin to rise. The light around you intensifies, but you find you're able to keep your eyes open with no discomfort. The walls of the tube melt away, and once again, you're floating weightlessly and free, although this time you're spared the accompanying stomach issues. In fact, you've never felt so utterly comfortable and at peace.

You realize that the warm glow that envelops you is more than just light—it's *thought*, a disembodied consciousness that gently merges with your own and speaks to you wordlessly in a warm, reassuring tone.

"OH MY GOD, I CAN'T BELIEVE YOU'RE FINALLY HERE!" it says. "IT'S BEEN WHAT, FOUR HUNDRED YEARS? BUT ALSO, LIKE, INFINITY? JESUS CHRIST, BEING THE ALL-KNOWING, SELF-AWARE EXPRESSION OF EXISTENCE IS A PAIN IN THE ASS."

Okay, that wasn't what you were expecting.

"OKAY, OKAY, WE DON'T HAVE MUCH TIME. WHAT DO YOU NEED TO KNOW HERE? OH, TRUST KRIKRI, SHE'S THE BEST! ALSO, DON'T START THE REBELLION IN THE MIDDLE AGES—WAIT, BUT IF YOU'RE HERE I GUESS YOU NEVER GO TO THE MIDDLE AGES. OR DO YOU? SO MANY VARIANTS!"

You're having a little trouble following this. "OH, AND

(continue to the next page)

YOU DEFINITELY NEED PROFESSOR V. TO STOP THE COMET IN THE CRETACEOUS! SHE MAKES THE SHIELD TO KEEP THEM OUT! I GUESS YOU NEED CHANCE TOO, BUT MOSTLY YOU NEED PROFESSOR V. PROMISE ME YOU'LL GET HER!"

A shield? To keep *who* out? "Um, okay. I promise."

"GOOD, GOOD. WHOA, IT LOOKS LIKE YOU'RE PHASING OUT. WAIT! THE KEY TO STOPPING THE INTERDIMENSIONAL TIME GOBLINS IS…"

The voice fades away, and you find yourself back in the tube, trying to come to terms with what just happened. Huh. That was super weird. The hatch opens, and you find the woman in the silver jumpsuit waiting. She seems more than a little surprised to see you and clasps both of your hands in hers.

"Isn't it wonderful?" she says. "Of course, the human mind can't wrap itself around anything more than the tiniest sliver of the Great Consciousness, so you only get snippets of images and vague impressions."

Apparently, surviving a visit with the Persistent Universe is the ticket to better treatment in 2271. "I've spent years meditating on my own audience," she says. "What did you see? Tell me everything!"

Somehow you doubt that "an excitable, disembodied voice rambling in all caps" is what passes for a religious experience in these parts. Or maybe this is some sort of test. Should you come clean? Or pretend that your experience was the life-changing metamorphosis this woman seems to expect?

▶ *If you tell her the truth,* **turn to page 257.**

▶ *If you tell her what you think she wants to hear,* **turn to page 171.**

"Just relax, and everything's going to be fine," Krikri says, calmly removing the hand from her shoulder. You stop baring your enormous teeth, and the clones each take a step backward. The nice thing about gatherings of identical doppelgangers is that they tend to react as a unit, and this one appears universally charmed by Krikri's earnest, soothing tones.

"Stop! Stop everything!" someone shouts from inside the camp. One of the duplicates is running toward you. His unkempt, graying beard and tattered lab coat are matched perfectly with the rest of the crowd, but something in his eyes looks haunted, like he just watched his dog die or something. At

(continue to the next page)

least he's not muttering gibberish under his breath or swatting at imaginary flies.

"It's broken!" he says. "I mean, it's perfect, it's fully operational, but just for a second, I understood. The whole plan is broken. *But I can fix it!* If I can remember, I can fix it."

His ranting is starting to rile the rest of the mob back up again. "And we can help you fix it," Krikri says. "Are you in charge here?"

"No one's in charge! There's no leader! I mean, we're all the leader, but I'm *three* leaders." He clenches his eyes shut and shakes his head as if trying to dislodge the crazy. "I know how that sounds. But just for a second, it all made sense."

"It's all right, Hercule," Krikri says. "Take your time."

"Hercule," he says, his eyes growing wide. "*He used to call me Hercule.*"

The scientist is cut off by a loud screech and a flash of light, and suddenly you're confronted by a rugged looking man in a leather jacket, dismounting from a futuristic motorcycle right in the middle of the jungle.

"I've got a report of unauthorized, time-shifted duplicates," he says in a vaguely European accent that's hard to place. Belgian, maybe? He's sporting a truly unfortunate mullet, but his physique is impressive, and he carries himself with the confidence of a Bengal tiger. "Time license and time registration, please."

You're certainly not carrying any paperwork. "Who are you supposed to be?" you ask.

"Chance Bruxelles, Time Patrol." He clicks his tongue and makes a little finger-gun gesture with one hand. Then he looks

(continue to the next page)

around the encampment and gives a low whistle. "Good lord, that's a lot of time-shifted duplicates. I'm going to have to take the whole lot in for questioning."

"No!" The slightly-less-insane clone that you've been calling Hercule is getting more agitated. "You have to let me figure this out! It's broken, but I can fix it if you just give me time!"

"You can fix everything back at the station," Bruxelles says. "We'll get all of you guys sorted out. Don't make this harder than it has to be, my friend."

"But if I do nothing, it's *so* much worse. Oh God, the destruction. If I do nothing, *everything* breaks!"

Huh. That doesn't sound great. "Maybe we should hear him out," you say.

Bruxelles' jaw stiffens. "I have no beef with you, friend. Stay out of this and let's keep it that way, yes?" He rubs his palms together and stares at you intently, like this isn't the first time he's had to take down a seven-ton Tyrannosaurus rex using mixed martial arts.

Maybe you should just let him round up the scientists and be done with it. It sounds like he's got jurisdiction here, anyway. Something about Hercule's ranting has you worried, though. And anyway, you're a freakin' *T. rex*. You should be able to take one guy in a leather jacket, right?

▶ *If you let the officer do his job,* **turn to page 96.**

▶ *If you insist that Bruxelles back off until you figure out what Hercule is gibbering about,* **turn to page 280.**

THIS ENTIRE PEASANT REBELLION WAS A TERRIBLE IDEA.

You're committed now, though. If you refuse to surrender, some good might still come of all this, right? Like, citizens across the country standing up and refusing to be treated so poorly? Even a loss here could be worthwhile if it inspires the masses.

It isn't. And it doesn't. If anything, it reminds the citizenry to accept their miserable lot because the alternative is getting slaughtered like livestock on the battlefield. Oh, and another tip? Don't trust commanders who look like talking dogs or lizards. Although "animal generals don't lead to victory, only disembowelment" definitely winds up being one of the weirder proverbs to enter the English language.

Oh, and you get captured and disemboweled, by the way. So it kind of made sense at the time.

The End

You're with Cartwright on this one. If dinosaurs were meant to fly… well, technically some of them *were*, but you aren't one of them. The two of you manage to persuade the gang—much to Annie's disappointment—to stick with the original plan.

As prepared as the group is for an assault on the compound, Annie needs time to incorporate the new data into their plans. It's well into the evening by the time she's ready. She loads up with a gadget that she calls a sensitrometer, which detects different energy signatures, and a sack full of electrical grenades designed to disrupt those specific types of energy. Cartwright, Bobbins, and the kids gear up with a variety of ornate, beautifully designed weapons. They let you have your pick, and you choose something appropriately badass.

The attack itself, however, proves anticlimactic. The front door of the compound is guarded by a single clockwork centurion, which detonates along with the greater part of the wall when the Powder Monkeys set off their explosives. Once inside, the few guards you encounter turn tail and run on sight before you even get the chance to shoot at them.

You make your way to a central control room, where the doors slam shut behind you moments after you step inside. A big, round trap door springs open in the center of the room, but Annie is prepared for it. Holding out her gizmo, she quickly selects a grenade and tosses it down the hole. There's a loud buzzing, followed by something that sounds like a slow-motion car crash.

"What was that?" you ask.

Annie smiles. "You don't even want to *know*."

You finish exploring the compound, but the nefarious

(continue to the next page)

sisters are nowhere to be found. You do discover, however, that the third floor includes an enormous, retractable roof. "Well, isn't that marvelous?" Bobbins says as he pulls a lever and watches the ceiling open up like the iris on a camera lens. "Hello, what's this? I've never witnessed a moon so…"

He trails off. You look up and immediately shield your eyes from the unexpected brightness. That's no moon. Something smaller and much more luminous is shining down on you, and as you squint at it, you realize its *below* the clouds. "What is it?" you ask to nobody in particular.

Annie points the sensitrometer at the sky. "My God!" she says. "Whatever it is, the power—it's off the dial! The device can't even *measure it.*"

"So, a lot," you say.

Her eyes widen. "You don't understand how much energy I built this thing to measure," she says. "That much power—it could be enough to destroy all of Chicago!"

Actually, it's enough to destroy all of *North America*. There's a blinding flash, which you don't even see since your eyes are incinerated along with the rest of your body the instant it happens.

We told you the good stuff was on the secret airship.

THE END

Who knows what could happen if you leave a twenty-first century Labrador running wild in prehistoric times? Everything you've learned about time travel is clearly meaningless, which means that any tiny alteration could have disastrous consequences in the future. That dog is rambunctious, too. Realistically, Betsy ending up in the belly of a rampaging dinosaur is probably the safest possible outcome for the security of the space-time continuum.

That doesn't mean you can bear to watch it, though. You turn your nebulous, metaphorical back on the impending carnage and set about finding a suitable host for your floating consciousness.

But something isn't right. You're used to drifting effortlessly on your way to a host body, but here, all movement is like swimming upstream. To make things worse, you already feel yourself losing your foothold in this reality. Instead of being pulled back into your native time period, though, you're just sort of... *dissipating*. You need to get yourself into a body—any body—fast!

▶ *If you take the quickest route and get yourself back into Betsy,* **turn to page 16.**

▶ *Wait, isn't Betsy about to be dinosaur lunch? If you make for the T. rex,* **turn to page 34.**

▶ *If you're committed to muddling on and finding a third option,* **turn to page 234.**

Okay, we're going to tell you straight up that this one doesn't end well. And it's not because the castle is well guarded against that sort of invasion (which it is). Or because, between your startling appearance and lumbering physique, you're remarkably ill-suited for stealth missions (which you are).

It's because Fleck's entire plan revolves around scaling the castle walls with grappling hooks, and your particular species of dinofolk *can't climb ropes*.

You arrive at the king's residence in the dark of night, and Boris and Fleck scurry up the stonework as quick as you please, but you're stuck at the bottom. Your tiny arms can't possibly support your weight, and any attempt to compensate with your jaws only results in cutting the line with your razor-sharp teeth. Your attempt at scaling the walls is utterly humiliating.

Also, quite loud. The castle guard is alarmed to find a vaguely dragon-shaped creature dressed all in black, reliving its worst day of middle school gym class.

They shoot you with crossbows.

THE END

You manage to get a leg through the first rift, hook your foot on something solid, and yank yourself from the void. Gravity reasserts itself from an unexpected direction and you fall to the ground, twisting your ankle in the process. You find yourself on a damp cobblestone street sometime after dark, sprawled over what looks like the wreckage of a big, steam-powered machine.

Hmm. Well, that's not so bad. Interdimensional time goblins are scurrying in and out of reality, chittering wildly in reaction to some invisible force only they can sense. But you'll take a smattering of the vile creatures on a city street over a whole swarm of them floating in a void any day. You pick yourself up carefully, trying not to put too much pressure on your—

BOOM.

Okay, that particular hole led to the epicenter of an explosion so massive it destroyed an *entire continent*. So you're dead. Feel free to head back to page 213 and see where the other ones go, if you want.

But it's not like they get better. Just so you know.

THE END

Annie rigs you up with a remote sensor device that she says will collect vital information about the compound's defenses. It fills the inside of a giant Victorian hat, has gears and antennae sticking out of it at all angles, and weighs about eighty-five pounds. You're expected to put it on your head.

"Um, you don't think they'll pick up on the fact that I'm wearing a wire?" you ask.

"Not to worry," Annie says with a grin. "Affixing useless gears and thingamabobs to one's clothing is the latest fashion. They'll *adore* it."

Even with your thick Tyrannosaurus neck musculature, you've got a crick like nobody's business by the time you reach the sisters' compound in the center of town. You politely inform the guards at the front gate—large, unwashed gentlemen who have had various appendages replaced with clockwork robot parts—that you have business with their superiors. They repay your courtesy by immediately tying you up with ropes.

In other words, the infiltration is coming together nicely so far. They haul you into a round room that appears to be some kind of control center. A well-dressed, raven-haired woman is seated at a console. She swivels in her chair as you enter, and her face lights up.

"Cornelia!" she yells to someone in the other room. "They found another lizard thing! It's much smaller than the last one—ooh, and it's wearing a top hat!"

Another one? "Excuse me," you say, "but there seems to have been a bit of a misunderstanding."

"Cornelia, it talks!" She claps her hands. "The other one didn't talk, did it?"

(continue to the next page)

"No, Beatrice, I believe it did not." A second woman enters the room, as elegantly dressed as the first, platinum blonde curls framing her face beneath an extravagant hat. Sure enough, there's an intricate network of cogs glued to it.

"Perhaps it would like to tell us," the second woman says without a hint of a smile, "why it blew up our jail this morning."

You launch into your carefully planned explanation—the Gas Can Rebellion was responsible for the explosion, you have valuable information about their whereabouts and intentions— but Cornelia cuts you off. "We have no interest in hearing stories about Gearbox Annie and her little band of reprobates," she says. "They remain irrelevant as ever."

She takes a few steps toward you and taps your time travel bracelet with a gloved finger, which of course results in a painful shock. "This, however, fascinates me," she purrs. "You wouldn't happen to be a visitor from the future, would you?"

You tense up, not sure how much of the truth you should tell her. These two have been acquiring the technology to build clockwork robots and body parts from somewhere—could they have dealings with other time travelers? Or be time travelers themselves? "The future? Er… that's crazy! What makes you ask?"

She backs away from you. "I require that device," she says to one of the thugs holding your restraints. "Horse, cut its arm off."

"Sure thing," the guard—whose name, apparently, is Horse—says. "You want I should shoot it first or just hack the thing off while it squirms?"

"Surprise me."

"Wait, wait, wait!" you say, panicking. "I'm *totally* from the

(continue to the next page)

future! And there's way more technology like this back where I come from! I can get it for you! Just don't cut my arm off!"

"That's more like it," she says. "Surely, we can discuss this like civilized people. Horse, untie our guest. And fetch some refreshments. Beatrice, what was it that the other one ate?"

"Whole cattle!" her sister says.

"Well, perhaps some sweetmeats then," Cornelia says. "And tea. Now, where shall we begin?"

You tell her you're new in this time period and would be happy to exchange information about future events for a basic rundown of their operation here in Chicago, since it doesn't even remotely match what's in your history books.

"Yes, of course," Cornelia says. "You're not the first visitor we've had from other ages. We're happy to get you situated. I believe there's more we can do for each other than that, however."

"Oh?" You're keenly aware that her guards are still looming, but at least this is better than being tied up.

She pulls a tiny key from a chain around her neck. "Show us how to use the time machine on your wrist," she says. "And loan it to us for one minute. You'll get it right back, fully operational. After that, you're free to go."

It does sound like an amazing deal. These two may be brutal dictators, but it's not like life for the average resident of Chicago in the 1880s was a paradise in your reality. Anyway, these mammal-folk are pretty evolved, so whatever it was that wrecked the dino-timeline clearly happened eons ago. You'll definitely need your time bracelet operational to fix it.

▶ If you agree to Cornelia's terms, **turn to page 27.**

▶ If you stick with the original plan and only commit to exchanging information, **turn to page 214.**

You surprise your assailant by sweeping its legs with your tail, causing it to lose its footing and topple backward into the portal. Excellent work! You briefly consider whether you should follow it, but before you can give it much thought, it comes popping right back out again.

Only now it's somehow been transformed into flesh and blood, just like you.

What the heck? Apparently that wasn't a time portal at all, but a *turn-mechanical-dinosaurs-into-regular-dinosaurs* portal. It closes back up, which is a shame because now you really want to know if going through it yourself would have turned you into a robot.

Your opponent looks utterly baffled by this turn of events, which is fine by you. After all, you already know how to deal with *regular* dinosaurs. You pounce, tearing its throat out before it has the chance to get its bearings and do the same to you. It may sound harsh, but tyrannosaur fights are not *tea parties*, you guys.

You've had about enough of this place. And although you're not sure if your own time machine is still functioning after your time in stasis, you know how to find out. You dig into the flesh of your fallen foe with abandon, eating as quickly as you can in hopes of indigestion.

As you gorge, a man bounds down the stairwell and into the chamber. He's decked out in a frock coat and a bowler hat with goggles on the brim, but you'd recognize his wild-eyed expression and unkempt beard anywhere. It's the mad scientist! Wait, didn't you eat that guy back in the Cretaceous? He quickly throws a series of switches, which opens a second chamber on

(continue to the next page)

the far side of the room. Apparently, this one is designed for travel rather than stasis, because he leaps into it and disappears.

You give a surprised little hiccup, and as if on cue, a time portal opens right in the middle of the mysterious chamber. The blue glow you've grown accustomed to interacts with the red light inside and becomes a kind of neon purple. Is it safe to go through? These things only remain open for seconds, so you'd better decide quickly.

Compounding your troubles, you hear a loud clattering from the stairwell. "Warning! Surrender or suffer the full force of law!"

▶ *You know what? We're not even going to give you a choice here. The steampunk 1800s suck, and you're getting the hell out of them.* **Turn to page 150.**

The Earth's atmosphere may make for a rocky landing, but it also guarantees that you'll be able to *breathe* once you get there, so you decide it's worth the risk. Your oxygen holds out, and when you hit atmosphere, your ship shakes like crazy but stays together. Krikri manages a reasonably well-controlled crash landing in front of the building that houses the Time Travel Investigation Agency. (You figured that stood a better chance of still existing in the year 2271 than your apartment, which was the only other place that came to mind when she asked for a specific destination.)

The building—in fact, the entire city—is completely abandoned. That can't be good. From what you've read in the TTIA's records, this entire region should be a bustling metropolis right up until…

Uh oh. "Krikri, what's today's date?"

She checks a display built into the glove of her outfit. "August 18th, 2271. Why?"

Six days after the 12th, which is the *furthest any TTIA agent has ever traveled and returned to tell the tale*. Is this why? Some sort of global catastrophe? You don't find any piles of corpses, which is reassuring, and the only hint of destruction is the mess you made of the asphalt on impact. All the people are simply *gone*.

The building still has power (and still has the same uninspired watercolor landscapes hanging on the walls from 250 years ago, which is weirdly comforting). But although they still power on, you can't get any of the screens set into the walls and furniture to display anything.

It's *super* creepy.

(continue to the next page)

You were hoping to find some version of your time travel bracelet here, but Professor V.'s secret back room has been converted to what might be a museum, and the only technology on display is the old Bakulan time travel rig, virtually unchanged from when last you saw it. Your heart sinks. Without any way of leaving this time period, your future looks pretty bleak.

Krikri, however, is fascinated by the entire concept of Bakulan time travel. "So you can use this to enter the bodies of those in other eras and experience the world from their perspectives? It sounds like the *ideal* method of gathering intelligence."

You decide to use the equipment to continue your mission, partly because it's the only avenue available and partly because Krikri seems interested, and you're eager to keep her around since, as far as you can tell, you're the only two people alive on the planet. You show her the basic functions of the machine and strap yourself in. Soon, your consciousness is back in the mad scientist's shabby little suburban home in 1983, about a month before your previous visit. You quickly locate Betsy, the faithful Labrador retriever who proved the perfect vantage point the last time you were here.

As you guide your consciousness toward the dog, however, the scientist himself enters the room. Hmm. TTIA rules warn against inhabiting the minds of the people you're sent to observe since their thoughts and feelings can theoretically color your perception. But if there was ever a time to ignore protocol, this is it.

▶ *If you play it safe and camp out in Betsy,*
   turn to page 188.

▶ *If you enter the mind of the scientist,*
   turn to page 52.

No one says anything outright, but you begin to suspect that your self-preservation instinct (or cowardice) isn't going over terribly well among your colleagues. For starters, you're assigned to "Fodder Squadron," which you don't love the sound of. Also, when the officers come around distributing laser rifles to your fellow troops, they just hand you a big metal stick. "No way!" someone says from behind you. "An authentic 1880s steampunk shock rod? I am truly jealous, my friend."

You turn to see a fresh-faced young man with an impressive physique and an even more impressive mullet. "Chance Bruxelles, Time Patrol," he says, sticking out one hand. "Hey, we haven't met before, have we?"

Before you can offer to trade Chance his raygun for your really cool stick, a massive portal opens in front of you. Someone barks an order, and you're swept through the threshold as your regiment marches forward. What you find on the other side is utter chaos. Twisted, howling goblin creatures are everywhere, swarming faster than your comrades can shoot them down. One latches onto your leg. Aaaah! Hit it with your stick! Hit it with your stick!

A burst of electricity erupts from the end of your staff on contact, and the creature lets out a screech and falls to the floor, smoking. Wow. That *is* pretty cool. You manage to hold your own in the melee and join a contingent battling its way toward the base's central chamber where the gateway to the Great Consciousness is housed. Things aren't looking good. Enemy forces seem endless while allies are dropping like flies. In fact, by the time you reach the goblins' force field, it's down to you, Velox, Krikri, Chance Bruxelles, and the guy with the Labrador head.

(continue to the next page)

"Damnit, Jurassic Squadron!" Velox yells through clenched teeth. "What are you *doing* out there?"

As if on cue, the energy field crackles and dissipates. Hooray! You follow Velox and Krikri into the chamber while Chance and Dog Guy situate themselves in the doorway, attempting to stem the goblin tide. The room is filled with big pneumatic tubes that serve as transport throughout the base. Velox rushes toward the one marked "Up."

"We must commune with the Great Consciousness!" she says. "It will know what to do!" The tubes are each lit from inside with a bright white light, and you notice that the light in Velox's is sputtering and turning a sickly yellow.

"I'm afraid we might be too late for that," Krikri says.

"What other option do we have?"

"The central power core." She gestures to a tube that's simply marked "Down." Apparently, the Temporal Custodians aren't big on specificity in their labeling system. "Blowing the core might cause an explosion big enough to take out all the goblins at once."

Might? You're not thrilled with her plan, both because she seems uncertain as to its effectiveness and because *avoiding* certain death was the whole point of skipping the suicide mission. Before you can raise these concerns, though, you hear screaming from the doorway, and goblins rush into the chamber.

Whatever you're going to do, you need to do it now.

▶ *If you jump in the tube marked "Up" and commune with that Great Consciousness,* **turn to page 293.**

▶ *If you choose the "Down" tube and end this adventure with a bang,* **turn to page 66.**

You get what Von Krumpf is trying to do here, but risking your life to help him prevent you and everyone you've ever known from ever being born seems like a lot to ask. You tell him to send you back to the TTIA offices in your own time period. You'll have to do quite a bit of explaining when you get there (and a lot of scrunching to get your new body through the corridors), but you're hoping Professor Venkataraman can help. As you enter the portal, however, you immediately discover that you're not alone.

Here's the thing about interdimensional time goblins: they feed on tachyon energy and lie waiting in the corridors of time looking for travelers to ambush, sucking their time machines dry. Normally, they would have no interest in attacking someone who's drifting through a portal and not carrying any kind of tachyon-emitting machinery. This bunch, however, just

(continue to the next page)

returned from an alternate dimension where a dinosaur fitting your description stayed in the Cretaceous period to fight them and ate roughly a hundred and fifty of their friends.

They're pretty cheesed about it.

The little buggers are much stronger in their own element, too. Hundreds of tiny, gnarled hands grab at you, and since you're basically in freefall, there's very little you can do to defend yourself. You roar in pain as they start tearing chunks of flesh off your bones. In a last-ditch Hail Mary attempt, you detach your consciousness from your dinosaur host.

Your thoughts go fuzzy as your awareness starts to dissipate into the timestream. What even *happens* to a disembodied mind hurtling through a physical time portal?

▶ **Turn to page 9** *to find out.*

Wow. You are *hardcore*. The truth is, you've got bigger things to worry about than adorable Labrador pups scampering around the Mesozoic era. (Seriously, wait 'til you meet the inter-dimensional time goblins.) But your commitment to temporal integrity is admirable, nevertheless.

You locate a suitably deadly volcano and prepare to hurl yourself in. Betsy, however, has other ideas. The mother's instinctive drive to protect her unborn children proves more powerful that your cold, calculating will, and in a fit of psychic self-preservation, her mind overwhelms yours. Betsy takes control of your combined persona and pushes you so deep into her subconscious that soon you're nothing more than a few nagging doubts in an otherwise healthy Labrador psyche.

Forever.

You have the chance to do plenty of morally questionable things in this book, but combination suicide/pregnant dog murder is not one of them.

The End

Breakfast, it turns out, is a hearty dish that Crabbe calls "peasant stew." You're having trouble parsing their medieval colloquialisms, though, so you assume he means "pheasant." It's a little gamey but quite filling. They convince you to join their troupe and dub you "Ye Fantastick Serpent Wot Talks." Your schtick is lounging in a cage which is decorated like a sitting room and hamming it up for the yokels, alternating between erudite conversation and animalistic roars. It's quite fun. Your understanding of Olde English improves as well—from their conversations, you glean that other terms for "traveling performer" in this era include "cutthroat" and "highwayman."

As you're preparing for a show on the third day, you're startled by a shimmering portal that appears in mid-air near your cage. A bald mammal-woman in a silver jumpsuit steps out of it.

"We need your help," she says. "The interdimensional time goblins are mounting their final assault on our moonbase in 2271, and I'm gathering errant time travelers to join the fight."

Before you can even begin to process this, Crabbe comes rushing toward you. "Dragon!" he screams.

"Yeah?"

"No! A PROPER dragon! Like you, but vast. And ferocious! 'Tis tearing up the countryside! Only you can save us!"

The jumpsuit woman sighs. "Remain here if you prefer," she says. "I have others to collect."

This could be your only chance to escape this century! You were just settling in with your new friends, though. Can you abandon them in their hour of need?

▶ *If you go with the jumpsuit woman,* **turn to page 261.**

▶ *If you stay in the Middle Ages and investigate Crabbe's dragon claims,* **turn to page 159.**

You thank Annie for the jailbreak, but her fight isn't yours. The Gas Can Rebellion convinces you to stay for lunch and hooks you up with a passable—if hastily tailored—1880s wardrobe. Since they've never seen dinofolk before, they clearly have no idea if you're male or female and seem embarrassed to ask, but they're good folks nonetheless.

From what you've observed, the various time travel shenanigans in this century don't have anything to do with your mad scientist, so your next move is to figure out a way to fix your time machine and move on to the next temporal activity cluster. Surely, somebody out there can help you! You decide that your best bet is making inquiries at the local tavern. Stealthily. On the downlow. As far under the radar as possible.

Unfortunately, things don't work out quite like you're hoping. After you escaped from the sisters' jailhouse, they put a bounty on your sizable head, and their minions have just finished spreading the news to this particular establishment that a hefty forty dollar reward will go to any citizen who brings in the talking dinosaur, dead or alive. That's more than nine hundred and fifty bucks when adjusted for inflation! The moment you step through those swinging saloon doors, you hear a collective gasp, followed by gunfire from every patron who hopes to nab a piece of the reward money.

They wind up having to split it twenty-six ways.

THE END

Maybe it won't be so bad! Ooh, what if they have a *Labyrinth*-style Goblin King? You'll take a magnificent package over a scrotum beard any day. Hmm. What is it about Goblin Kings and genitalia, anyway? As you ponder this, the gnarled creatures close in.

"Uh, take me to your leader?"

They do not. I'm not saying you would have fared better in the evil energy cloud (the truth is, you were pretty much screwed the moment you set foot in the mothership), but the reception you get is NOT pretty. Like, what do a bunch of mindless goblin creatures even WANT with twenty-five feet of dinosaur entrails? They don't eat. Are they decorating for a party or something?

You're super dead, so you never find out.

THE END

If some other mysterious, floating consciousness wants a dinosaur to ride around in, it can damn well find its own. Chompy is yours and yours alone!

(We should probably mention at this point that you've taken to thinking of your murderous, rage-filled Tyrannosaurus rex host as "Chompy.")

The rival entity, however, is *really* good at calming dinosaurs and starts to assume control. You won't stand for that! You've spent the last half hour trying to keep your most savage, carnivorous instincts bottled up, but now you embrace the beast and let your fury flag fly. You're untamable! You're wild! But most of all? You're frickin' *hungry*.

You snap at the dolphin with your massive jaws, but she sees you coming and disappears in the blink of an eye. Hmm, that's a neat trick. Undeterred, you sniff the air and launch yourself across the landscape toward the closest mass of edible-smelling animal meat. The other consciousness tries to stop you in your tracks, but it's too late for that. With a mighty roar, you focus all your rage into a sort of psychic brain blast and push the mysterious interloper out of your head. You did it!

Then the tyrannosaur immediately repeats this process, forcing your sorry ass out as well. Whoops. With no link to your own time zone or an active host body, your awareness briefly tumbles through the ether and dissipates. In moments, there's nothing left of you at all.

Goddamnit, Chompy.

THE END

Your instinct for self-preservation kicks in, and you wrestle your alternate self for the gun. Needless to say, the two of you are pretty evenly matched. In fact, for a battle between two Tyrannosaurus rexes, it's pretty uninspiring since neither of you have any hand-to-hand combat experience to speak of. Eventually, the gun goes off while it's sandwiched between the two of you, and you're shocked to find yourself spattered with your own blood. Well, technically, the blood of your time-shifted duplicate, but it's still gross. Your doppelganger falls to the floor with a thud.

"See, was that so hard?" Bruxelles asks. His own double seems to have left. "Wait—are you the future dinosaur or the past one?"

"The past one!"

"What? I think you are not clear on the entire concept of what we're trying to accomplish."

"It was self defense!"

"Okay, we're going to try this one more time." He grabs you and plops you down on the motorcycle seat behind him. "This time, just shoot him! You already did it once, so it should be easy."

"Wait! If I go back now, we already know what happens—the past me kills the future me. But this time I'LL be the future me!"

"Only because you hesitate," Bruxelles says. "Do not hesitate!"

With a flash and a squeal, you find yourself back in the room with two other copies of yourself, one in bed screaming and another turning toward you, surprised.

▶ *If you shoot that dinosaur,* **turn to page 147.**

▶ *If you hesitate,* **turn to page 279.**

Fortune favors the bold, right? You leap on the back of Chance's motorcycle just as it makes the jump, and a psychedelic laser show erupts around you. Moments later, you're in the middle of a large concrete room.

"Son of a bitch!" Chance says. "That was amazing! I've never seen someone ballsy enough to jump onto a timecycle in mid chrono-jump. You should have been killed!" He hops off his bike and shakes your tiny T. rex hand vigorously. "Have you ever considered a career in chrono enforcement?"

"Damnit, Bruxelles, what did I tell you about stealing that bloody prototype?" The woman who approaches is somewhat taller than Bruxelles and nearly as broad. She's also clearly mastered the art of the disapproving frown.

"That I might explode," Chance says. "But I didn't! Instead, I was the second person to ever travel past August 12, 2271. Captain Steele, meet my new partner. It's a talking dinosaur!"

She gives you a cautious nod. "Ah, I see you're a fellow time traveler," she says, glancing at your bracelet. You don't tell her that the thing is completely shot. Instead, you detail your experiences with Krikri, the Temporal Custodians, and the interdimensional time goblins.

"Well, if Bruxelles vouches for you, that's all the reference I need," she says. "At Time Patrol, we protect the timestream from all threats, foreign and domestic. Can I sign you up? I'm afraid it's either that or drop you off back where we found you. We can't risk potential damage to temporal stability by taking you anywhere else."

Back to 2271 is the last place you want to go.

▶ **Turn to page 198.**

All your memories are of the dino-universe, yet there's something about that monkey reality you can't quite put your finger on. Like, maybe there was a monkey version of you there at some point and a few stray tachyon particles are still clinging to you from that timeline? For whatever reason, you have an unshakable feeling that it's where you belong.

The featureless thought-void swirls around you, and you feel your essence start to dissipate with it. Yikes—did you just *unmake* yourself? Your consciousness fades out but then flips back on like a switch as you open your eyes. You find yourself back in the Time Travel Investigation Agency where all this began, strapped into the Bakulan time travel machine and looking up at Professor Venkataraman. Of course, you still remember her as Professor Velociraptor but recognize this version instantly. Something about her gentle, serene little mammal face just feels *right* to you.

She looks down at you and screams.

And that, my friend, is how you became a lone Tyrannosaurus in a world of sentient primates, protecting humanity from threats to the timeline without ever quite belonging to it yourself. A force for justice standing between order and chaos. The greatest Time Travel Investigation Agent the universe will ever know. How you became…

Time Travel Dinosaur.

THE END

You trust Chance. You kind of have to, at any rate—if you think you're badass enough to defeat even a smallish group of armed thugs while partially restrained, you need to start paying WAY more attention to this book. Your captors march you down a hallway toward a heavy-looking steel door. You look to your partner for some hint of a signal, but he seems calm and mildly oblivious. So you step out into the moonlight—

And a whirling maelstrom of double-fisted, roundhouse-kicking fury.

When the dust settles, all four goons are lying unconscious on the cobblestones, and you see Chance using a small laser to cut through the handcuffs of... another Chance. A second version of you comes to untie your restraints, which is an unsettling experience, both due to the shock of observing yourself from outside your own body and because your tiny arms are uniquely unsuited to the task. The two Chances, meanwhile, are busy executing an elaborate handshake that ends in a chest-bump.

"But...!" you stutter, still shaken by the experience. "How did you know we'd be here to save ourselves?"

"Because I always am," Chance says proudly. "Whenever I get into a tough scrape, I just remember to travel back and rescue myself afterwards. Works like a charm, every time."

You turn to your double. "So, you're *me*? From the future?"

The other you shrugs. "I might be the wrong person to ask. Professor V. sent me here, and I've just kind of been tagging along with this guy all day."

"There will be time to hash all this out back at HQ," Chance says. "We have a nefarious plot to foil! How do we get to the

(continue to the next page)

sisters' airship?"

"Strap yourselves to this," the other Chance says, patting the hull of what looks like an enormous steampunk missile, conveniently leaning against the building's wall. "I'll light the fuse, and off you go!"

It does *not* look safe. "How do we steer it?" you ask.

"You don't, really," Future Chance replies. "Don't worry, I'll aim it. I remember which way to point."

"Trust me!" Regular Chance says. "If that's how they did it, that's how we'll do it. They're us! Everything will be fine!"

Despite their unshakable confidence in predestination, you're having a tough time believing that you can just point a copper death trap toward some unseen destination above the clouds and somehow arrive safely. "We definitely both survive this, then?"

"Well, to be honest, I was a little afraid I'd lost you up there," Future Chance says. "But then I came back to look for my motorcycle, and here you were, safe and sound! It all worked out!"

Regular Chance is already tying one arm to the missile. "Hurry," he says. There's no time to lose!"

Something about this whole scenario is screwy as hell. But trusting Chance has worked out pretty well so far, right?

▶ *If you strap in,* **turn to page 258.**

▶ *If you insist on finding a less insane method of air travel,* **turn to page 67.**

Alas, it doesn't work like that at all. Has Professor Velociraptor taught you nothing? The universe, as she said, is pretty good at worming its way out of impossible paradoxes. If Chance Bruxelles is here with you now, shooting your sleeping, alternate self in the face out of the sheer kindness of his heart, he'll still wind up doing the same thing if he never meets you, probably because he's convinced you're a deadly threat to the timestream or something.

In fact, with the choices you've been making, you just might be. Bruxelles moseys on over to the bed, gives you a reassuring smile, aims his weapon, and pulls the trigger. Sometime in the middle of last week, you're murdered in your sleep.

You never saw it coming.

THE END

Yeah, you totally get yourself shot.

But wait! It isn't in vain! You leap into the line of fire just as the revolver discharges, taking the bullet that was intended for the merged clone. Your chest explodes in pain as your full weight smacks into Longbeard, knocking him backward, directly into the beam.

"Betsy! Noooooo!" The now triple-merged scientist rushes to your side. "What have I done? Oh, God—shut it down! Shut it all down!"

Thanks to your noble sacrifice, calmer (and marginally less insane) heads prevail, and the blue beam flickers out. Alas, this is the end of the line for you. But take comfort in the fact that without your actions here, the multiverse would certainly be doomed. Also, because the sheer volume of tachyon particles has destabilized the space-time continuum in the immediate vicinity, local timelines are merging in unpredictable ways. This means that another version of you, who made different decisions, could wander along at any moment to pick up the baton from your heroic, bleeding paws.

Wait for it… Wait for it…

Okay, you pretty much bleed out before any other yous show up to continue your adventure. Still, it *might* happen.

THE END

Suddenly, you're in the swirling vortex once again as the universe changes around you. You're beginning to seriously rethink your decision not to peel yourself off the space-time continuum because this *blows*. Hopefully, the tachyon particulate will wear off soon, so you can remain blissfully unaware of alterations to the timestream like normal people. (Technically, you're being dragged across alternate timelines by the tachyon bond that tethers you to the peeled-off scientist. But either way, it's getting old.)

You find yourself in a shadowy alley, hidden under a billowing cloak. You're wearing high-tech gauntlets, and your mask has night vision lenses, allowing you to see in the darkness as clear as day. A supervillain cowers before you.

Holy *ass-biscuits*. Are you *Batman* in this timeline?

"I didn't do nothin', I swear!" the villain whimpers. You recognize him as Rockjockey, a superpowered thug who has the ability to armor himself with bits of stone and masonry. He's obviously terrified and eager to talk. He tells you he's on the run from a retired superhero named Cosmic Guardian, who's now working for your long-time nemesis, Reginald Thorpe.

Before you can question him further, a text message flashes across your wrist screen. "SHUT DOWN YOUR SYSTEMS," it says. Your head is still foggy from the tachyons, but you seem to remember that you're not actually the real Batman here. And that the real Batman might be pissed at you?

▶ *If you obey the text message,* **turn to page 202.**

▶ *If you blow it off and continue your interrogation,* **turn to page 266.**

You know what? Screw it. If that other you wants to get shot stealing a motorcycle, fine. You back off, fully expecting things to turn murdery. Instead of drawing his weapon, though, Bruxelles launches into the air and knocks your doppelganger halfway across the room with a roundhouse kick. It's actually kind of amazing.

"Ah-ah-ah. Keep your grubby claws off the timebike, my friend," he says with a smirk. "I think now we know which one is the evil twin, yes?"

As your alternate self lies on the floor moaning, a column of light appears in the space between you. Out of the column steps a statuesque woman in a silver jumpsuit, her head completely shaved. She's another monkey person, but even so, you've got to admit she's rocking that outfit. *Damn.*

"Temporal Custodians!" Bruxelles yells, leaping behind his motorbike. "Take cover!"

(continue to the next page)

"What? I thought *you* were a Temporal Custodian."

"I'm a Time Patrol officer! Whole different thing!" He pulls you to the floor, even though it occurs to you that the motorcycle doesn't make a particularly good shield for a single person, let alone two.

Professor Velociraptor peeks her head out from behind a lab station. "Everyone just calm down. I'm sure we can work this out without resorting to violence."

"Indeed we can," the jumpsuited woman says in a measured tone. "Chance Bruxelles. It seems I'm here to clean up your mess once again."

"Velox!" Bruxelles shouts. He seems big on shouting. "As beautiful as the frozen tundra, and twice as cold! You may leave! I have everything under control here!"

"Of course you do," she says with a sigh. "Regardless, I'm taking both of them in for processing. Now step away from the duplicate before you make everything worse, as usual."

"You step away from *your* duplicate!" Bruxelles says. "Or I'll shoot!" He glances at you, and his eyes light up. "Or maybe I go ahead and shoot this dinosaur instead! Eh? What does your Persistent Universe think about that?"

Velox pauses for a moment, narrowing her eyes.

"I *loathe* you," she says at last. "Fine. I'm taking this one, but if I decide I need them both, I'll be back." The light column appears again, and in the blink of an eye, both she and your doppelganger are gone.

"WHAT THE HELL?" you say.

"Oh, sorry about that," Bruxelles says. "I wasn't really going to shoot you. A bluff to save your life! Those Temporal

(continue to the next page)

Custodians are bad news. They believe themselves to be agents of something they call the Persistent Universe, and they use time travel to make the timestream the way they think it would be if no one used time travel at all."

That makes a kind of sense, you suppose. "What do you guys do at the Time Patrol, then?"

He flashes you a grin. "We catch bad guys! And trust me, nobody they take in for 'processing' ever re-enters the timestream. Which is a shame, because we could really use a pair of Tyrannosaurus people in the fight against evil. But I suppose one will do! Come with me back to Time Patrol HQ— you'll be safe from the custodians there. Are you peeled off?"

"Am I what?"

"Peeled off of the space-time continuum. You know, the whole killing yourself in the past to create an impossible paradox business. I can't take you with me unless you've done this first."

The officer gets on his motorcycle and looks at you expectantly. That Velox woman said she might be back for you at any moment—if Time Travel HQ is a way to avoid "processing," whatever that is, it sounds good to you. Should you lie to Bruxelles? What's the worst that could happen if you do?

▶ *If you tell the officer you've been peeled off the space-time continuum,* **turn to page 84.**

▶ *If you admit that you're still very firmly attached to it,* **turn to page 260.**

You're not proud of it, but when it comes down to a choice between your life and the lives of two medieval townsfolk— regardless of their kind deeds and adorable urchin-ness—you're looking out for number one. As soon as the child leaves, you sneak out of the barn and run as fast as your powerful dinosaur legs can carry you, which is actually pretty fast. Before long you've left the town (and, for the most part, your terrible, nagging guilt) far behind.

Now the sun is going down, and the air grows chilly. You keep traveling, hoping to stumble upon something you can eat or disguise yourself with, but have no luck. The only thing anybody seems to farm around here is dirt, and the clothesline conveniently hung with cozy blankets that you pictured in your head never materializes. Hours into the evening, your exhaustion finally grows stronger than your hunger or your chill, and you find a secluded spot under some brush away from the road and fall asleep.

It's not quite secluded enough, however. The following morning, you're awakened by something poking you in the stomach.

"It's alive!" someone says, prodding you again. "Ooh, and it's right hideous, too."

"Quit it!" you mutter, still mostly asleep. You vaguely remember your older sister waking you up by poking you with things when you were young. "Mom! Vanessa's poking me!"

You finally pry open your eyes and see two men in robes looking down at you. They look nothing like your sister Vanessa. The larger one has a big, heavy stick in one hand, though, which explains the poking.

(continue to the next page)

"And it speaks!" the big one says. The smaller man stretches up on his toes and whispers something in his companion's ear, but the big man just looks confused. "You think?" he asks. The smaller man whispers again, and this time the big man's eyes widen. He smiles, drops his stick, and reaches underneath his robe for something. If he's going for a weapon, you're in trouble. You try to scramble to your feet but slip on the scattered leaves and vegetation you had been using as a bed. You fall squarely on your tail, completely at the mercy of the robed duo.

Sure enough, what emerges from beneath the man's cloak is a big, nasty-looking blade. He proceeds to stab you. A lot.

"Toby says you must be the talking dragon/demon creature that was supposed to fight Lord Fenwick at dawn," you hear him say as the life drains out of you. "The price on your head is worth as much as the whole Freakporium put together!"

You never get the chance to ask what a Freakporium is.

THE END

You didn't get where you are in life by *not* leaping blindly into mysterious portals. For the second time today, you find yourself hurtling through the timestream, but this time, no power in the 'verse is going to knock you out of your host body because NOTHING IS BETTER THAN BEING A DINOSAUR.

You find yourself in a lush, grassy field with a low stone wall stretching the length of it. A squat, dirt-encrusted woman is pulling a handcart along the path, but takes one look at you, drops her cart and runs screaming. You're sort of hoping that her abandoned cart is full of pies or something, but upon further inspection, it's only dirt. Seriously? Who transports dirt in a cart? Like, wherever she's dragging that thing to doesn't already have *dirt*? You wander the open fields, and after scaring a few more peasants, come to the conclusion that you're somewhere in medieval Europe. Wait. One. Freaking. Second. You just realized what just might be EVEN BETTER than being a dinosaur.

Being a motherflippin' *dragon*.

You spend a solid week terrorizing the countryside and feasting on stray sheep. And it's *everything you never knew you wanted*. At one point some guy in ratty chainmail even trots out to meet you in battle, but with a single roar, you knock him off his steed and send him running with his tail between his legs. Then you eat his horse.

Life is good! The only thing missing is a hoard of gold—hmm, perhaps you could demand tribute from the townsfolk? You'd have to make sure they understood to just send cash and not, like, virgins or something. Come to think of it, though, those girls are probably better off with you than with any parents who would try to pay off a dragon with *their kids*. Maybe you should

(continue to the next page)

just accept any daughters they offer you? And try to teach them a trade or something?

As you're pondering the implications one evening, you see a line of torches marching up the hillside to your lair. What? Are the peasants mounting an attack? That's *adorable*. It's also a stroke of luck—a little frightful bellowing and the rubes will be willing to do anything to appease you. You'll have that hoard in no time!

You're so excited by the prospect that you burp up a bit of your mutton dinner, and a time portal appears on the hillside along with it. Hey! You figured you had digested that time machine days ago. Now, however, you have a decision to make. You're having the time of your life here. That doorway could send you anywhere in history. Is there any more wondrous place for a Tyrannosaurus rex than the Middle Ages?

Then again, you thought the same thing about the Cretaceous period.

▶ *If you take your chances with the time portal once again,* **turn to page 229.**

▶ *If life here is too good to pass up and you stay put,* **turn to page 59.**

You decide that do-overs are the better part of valor and hit the button on your armband, rolling sideways into the time portal to avoid a fourth pummeling from the clockwork terminator. You take the now-familiar trip through the timestream and pop back out in Professor V.'s lab, face-to-face with…

Aaaaaaaah! Monkey professor!

The woman before you is dressed exactly the same as Professor V. was the last time you saw her, but looks more like the 1880s children than the kindly, erudite raptoid that you know and love. Uh oh. Could your brief, largely pointless visit to the past possibly have changed the present *this* much? No, of course not. The 1880s weren't even a century and a half ago. Plus, the people were already monkeys when you got there.

"Um, Professor… *Velociraptor*?" you ask a little hesitantly.

"Venkataraman," she says, holding out a tiny little mammal hand that's barely even bigger than yours. "Do I know you?"

You explain, and although this version of the professor never sent her subordinate out to safeguard the timestream, she agrees that it does sound like her. Apparently, when you're a time machine inventor, stuff like this happens all the time. She helps you tend to your bruises and lacerations, and then it's back to the grindstone. After all, Temporal Activity Clusters aren't going to investigate themselves.

Where to next?

▶ *If you think it's time to check out the Cretaceous Period,* **turn to page 48.**

▶ *If you head for the future,* **turn to page 63.**

▶ *If you want another crack at the 1880s,* **turn to page 97.**

You fire the ancient revolver that Professor Velociraptor gave you and watch in horror as your mirror image howls in pain and starts coughing up blood. It's messy, it's ugly, and it's exactly the reason you wanted to avoid the whole alternate-self-murder thing in the first place.

What happens next, though, is even more terrifying. Whatever you imagined peeling yourself off the fabric of space-time might feel like, this is ten times worse. It's as if every single molecule in your body had its own place in the universe, a perfect little home where it belonged, and is now being forcibly evicted from that home while clinging to the doorframe, kicking and screaming. As your life rushes through your mind in vivid detail, you somehow realize that these memories now belong solely to you. They'll never again quite mesh with the rest of the universe, and all you can hope for is to settle into a timestream with as much overlap as possible.

Still dazed, you feel yourself being lifted off the floor and onto the timecycle. "Come on," Bruxelles says. "Once you start time jumping, it gets easier." The psychedelic laser show erupts around you, and moments later, you're in the middle of a busy street, surrounded by monkey-people with uniforms and haircuts similar to Bruxelles (even the women, although their mops of hair tend to be, on average, larger). The cars are angular and severe, much like the contraption you arrived on.

"What year is this?" you ask.

"2024," Bruxelles says proudly. That's only eight or nine years ahead of your own time—you have difficulty believing automobiles could have gotten *that* hideous *that* quickly. "Chief!" he shouts, flagging down someone he recognizes on

(continue to the next page)

the street. "I brought a talking dinosaur to help us patrol the timestream!"

The woman who approaches is taller than Bruxelles and nearly as broad. Her skin is also a significantly darker shade—so far the mammalians haven't displayed anywhere near the variety in decoration and coloring found in regular dinofolk, but it's nice to see a little variation. She looks you up and down for a moment, and you try your best not to wither under her gaze. Finally, she sticks out one hand.

"Captain Francesca Steele," she says. "Welcome to Time Patrol HQ."

Offering to shake hands with a tyrannoid, of course, is a huge faux pas in polite society. But she can't be expected to know that, you suppose. So you awkwardly lean your body toward her while averting your massive head, getting one little arm close enough to grasp her fleshy mammal paw. "Pleasure," you grunt back graciously. "Quite an impressive operation you've got here."

"Two hundred officers, the finest tech to be found in any era, and a temporal shield that keeps out unwanted guests," she says with pride. "You're damn right it's impressive. Time travelers in general tend to be a megalomaniacal, wretched lot, and it's our job to keep them from abusing the timestream for their own personal gain. Or worse, completely breaking the whole damn space-time continuum." You have to admit, Time Patrol sounds pretty badass.

"Officer Bruxelles is a goddamned idiot," Captain Steele continues, "but he's our best agent by far." Bruxelles makes a little gun-gesture with his fingers and gives you a wink. "Anyone

(continue to the next page)

he vouches for has a place with us. Mostly because, when he doesn't get his way, he sulks for a month and winds up being a giant pain in my ass. So what do you say? Can we get you in a badge and a leather jacket?"

"Remember, you're either with us or against us," Bruxelles chimes in helpfully.

Preventing madmen from destroying all of space-time is exactly what you're here for, and you could certainly use the help of a highly trained—if unfortunately mulleted—law enforcement organization. On the other hand, these are monkey-people, not dinofolk. Their idea of a "normal" timestream and yours aren't necessarily going to match up. If your mission is to restore the *real* timeline—the timeline where people evolved from *dinosaurs*—throwing your lot in with this crew might prove counterproductive. You still have your time machine wristband, so it's not like you're a prisoner here.

▶ *If you accept Captain Steele's offer to join the Time Patrol,* **turn to page 198.**

▶ *If you'd rather go it alone,* **turn to page 206.**

You leap headfirst into that crazy purple portal. Something is definitely wrong, though—this time the usual vertigo is accompanied by searing pain. It feels like every molecule in your body is trying to forcibly detach itself from every other molecule, and the experience is not pleasant. Fortunately, it's over soon.

You find yourself in the familiar confines of a prehistoric forest. Your memory is full of holes, like Swiss cheese—did you just come from somewhere in the 1800s? Or the Middle Ages? Suddenly, all that feels like a dream.

All you know for sure is that you have the mind of a human agent of the Time Travel Investigation Agency and the body of a savage, 20-foot tall Tyrannosaurus rex. In fact, you can barely seem to control the base instincts of your dinosaur body. And although you vaguely recall having eaten recently, you're absolutely famished. You look down and see that pesky scientist, back in his ratty lab coat, time machine still strapped to his chest.

The entire scene gives you an overwhelming sense of déjà vu. But right now, there's nothing in the world you want more than to eat that guy.

▶ *If you give in to temptation and chow down,*
turn to page 265.

▶ *If you hold off on lunch until you can figure out what's going on here,* **turn to page 78.**

You're new to this whole time portal business, and you concede that destroying your own time machine might have some unforeseen consequences. You relax and let the alternate version of yourself out of the sleeper hold.

"So long, sucker!" your doppelganger says, jumping head-first into the time portal.

Suddenly, you start to remember the past few minutes very differently. Professor Velociraptor was just starting to explain something to you about Bakulan and non-Bakulan time travel when another you jumped out of a portal and tackled you, talking all crazy about murder and paradox. Then you got free and jumped into the portal. For some reason, you *really* wanted to go through that portal. Then you encountered yourself and relived the experience from the opposite point of view.

Wow. Time travel is *the worst*.

"Killing your past self is the only way to separate your consciousness from the ever-changing timestream," Professor Velociraptor says. "We have to try again."

"Wait," you say. "Why the rush? It's *time travel*. Don't we have all the time in the world to work out a better plan?"

"Alas, no," she says. "When you witnessed that scientist's paradoxical event in 1983, you were inundated with tachyon particles. It formed a bubble around the two of you, but that bubble will dissipate quickly. For now, you're linked, but we must act fast. For all I know, we may already be too late."

She looks you in the eyes. "Are you ready?"

▶ If you tell her you'll try again, **turn to page 12.**

▶ If you've decided that murdering yourself is out of the question, **turn to page 14.**

You run for it, making good use of those mad ninja dog skills. The scientists follow, now seeming to come from every direction. Soon the forest is thick with wild-eyed lunatics, and you're not sure you can avoid capture for much longer. You head for the densest foliage in hopes of finding cover, but hear something ahead that's even more frightening than insane bearded guys in lab coats. The bushes are rustling and animals are screeching—you're pretty sure something (or a pack of somethings) is *feeding* over there. Could you lure your pursuers into the frenzy and somehow avoid being eaten yourself? Seems dicey.

Suddenly a streak of darkness appears to your left, as if reality itself was torn asunder. This doesn't look anything like the scientist's shimmering portals, though—it's jagged and misshapen, and you swear you can sense *waves of malevolence emanating from it.*

You're beginning to wish you'd just gone with the scientists into their stupid tower. It looks like that ship has sailed, though—chasing you has riled these guys to the point where you're ninety percent sure they're straight up going to kill you now.

So what's it going to be?

▶ *If you charge head first into what sounds like a dinosaur feeding frenzy,* **turn to page 201.**

▶ *If you dive into the rift in reality that's so evil and foreboding you can barely even stand to look at it,* **turn to page 68.**

You set your armband to jump a week into the past and push the button. An enormous portal, just big enough for your cramped, goblin-sized spacecraft to pass through, opens up ahead of you. Your ship passes through it…

And you find the entire interdimensional time goblin armada, assembled to prepare for its assault on the custodians' moonbase, waiting for you on the other side.

They open fire without even checking to see why one of their own half-wrecked ships would be emerging from a time portal. (Interdimensional time goblins, on the whole, are a twitchy lot.) You try to program your time machine for another jump but discover that creating a portal of that magnitude has completely fried it.

"We've lost navigation!" Krikri says. "And life support. I'm afraid there's no way out of this now." She leaves the console and comes to your side. "I'm going to go back and make sure you travel forward instead," she says. The ship is rocked by another blast, and you feel the air being sucked out of the room from some hole in some other area of the craft.

"We can still fix this, then! Everything will be fine!"

"You don't understand," Krikri says. "With every choice you make, the timeline splits and creates an alternate reality. So another version of you will travel to the future and hopefully survive. But here, now…"

She grasps both of your hands in hers. "I'm sorry." With a soft pop, Krikri is gone.

Then, with a deafening explosion, so are you.

The End

You're not sure what's going down back in 2271, but if forced to choose between the Time Patrol and the Temporal Custodians, you choose the ones with the awesome '80s hair. Velox disappears back into her lightbeam, and you turn your attention to the interdimensional time goblins.

You discover, much to your dismay, that they've multiplied. There are now six of the creepy little buggers, and as soon as Velox is gone, they pounce. They're stronger than they look and attach themselves to your head and face. (They leave your arms free, but those aren't long enough to be of much use in a wrestling match.) You're quickly overwhelmed.

Just as you think all is lost, you feel a jolt of electricity, and one of the goblins detaches from you. Several more shocks follow, and the rest of the goblins fall away. You see a man in period clothing with one arm made of clockwork and brass, like some kind or steampunk cyborg. *Steamborg*, maybe? He's joined by a woman with two metal legs and a man who's either wearing a helmet or has had his entire head replaced with clockwork.

Before you have a chance to thank your saviors, however, another electrical blast hits you square in the chest.

"Damn, these Timecopper bastards just get uglier and uglier," one of them says. This would be the Steampunk Mafia, then. They're armed with sticks that emit an electrical charge on contact. And they keep hitting you until you lose consciousness.

Because, you know. Free motorcycle.

THE END

Whatever's going on inside the brain of that savage beast, you want no part of it. You leave the tyrannosaur to battle with its monkey mind and settle into Krikri's shiny gray head instead.

You find her mind serene and welcoming. She knows you're there and offers you all her thoughts and memories openly. The first thing you realize is that Krikri isn't from an alternate reality at all. The dinofolk and the dolphin people *share the same timeline*. She comes from millions of years in your future, after dinosaurs became extinct due to a conflux of pollution, over-population, global warming, a polar reversal, and several truly unfortunate solar flares. Dolphins eventually evolve to walk on land and become the planet's dominant species, creating the kind of utopian society that your people have only dreamt of.

Krikri has much more to share with you, but unfortunately, the prehistoric dinosaur wins its psychic battle while you're distracted by wonders from the distant future and bites your collective head off.

That floating monkey consciousness could *really* have used your help.

THE END

You gyrate wildly and manage to get your face through one of the rifts, clamping down on a stray tree branch and pulling yourself through. You fall a couple of feet and hit a soft patch of ground. You seem to have landed in a lush tropical jungle. It's *beautiful*. What's that smell, though?

Oh—dead dinosaur. You turn to see a pack of dog-sized velociraptor-things devouring a much larger animal. Your sudden arrival startles them, and they pounce.

Still have your finger in that page?

AAAAAAAAAGH, THE PAIN IS EXCRUCIATING! THEY'RE TEARING THE FLESH OFF OF YOUR BONES AND FEASTING ON YOUR TENDER INSIDES! OH GOD, THIS IS EVEN WORSE THAN THE FIRST HOLE! WHY? WHYYYYYYYYYYYYYYYYY?

THE END

Before you can act on your carefully considered decision, the room is spinning again, and you find yourself in a mid-priced Italian restaurant, holding a tray of appetizers. Apparently, time traveling madmen alter the course of history like every five minutes around these parts. You wouldn't notice at all if you hadn't been inundated with the specific tachyon particulate of the original break.

Yes you would, a tiny voice calls out from somewhere deep in your consciousness.

You push that voice back down and get on with the task at hand, which is tray service. The stuffed bunny at table four has finally ordered, and you're bringing chicken wings, an order of sweetbread, and a stiff drink. Although you can't believe anybody actually orders the sweetbread here. It's the only thing on the menu more disgusting than the deep fried ravioli blasters.

Hold on. Did you just casually refer to a customer as a *stuffed bunny?* You look down and note that you're a completely normal human being. Could this be a reality where some people evolved from primates and others evolved from *plush toys?* You glance back at table four, and discover an even bigger surprise.

Apparently other people evolved from rotting corpses, because the bunny's date is clearly a zombie.

As confused as you are by residual tachyons, there's no way that can be normal. Seriously, how does the rabbit *not realize* it's on a lunch date with the living dead?

▶ *If you bring the couple their appetizers as if nothing was wrong,* **turn to page 138.**

▶ *If you run from the restaurant screaming,* **turn to page 202.**

Yeah! You show 'em! You manage to get enough control of your neck muscles to lash out and knock one of the automatons off its feet. The other one, though, responds by shocking you again. You keep thrashing around in defiance, so their sensors continue to register you as a threat, and the electric jolts just keep coming.

Eventually they just sort of cook you on the spot.

Which is good news for the hooligans and thugs who have taken to calling themselves the Steampunk Mafia. Ever since the Shaughnessy sisters seized control of the city, they've been all about exotic meats.

Let me tell you, they eat *well* tonight.

THE END

Crabbe and Toby's Wondrous Freakporium is your home now, and you won't leave your companions to be eaten by... *dragons*? Those things didn't actually exist in the Middle Ages, did they? You rush to the edge of the camp just in time to see the beast snatch up a couple of sheep and disappear over the hillside. Your vantage point isn't ideal, but it looks more like a prehistoric tyrannosaur than a dragon. Millions of years before they evolved into modern tyrannoids, your ancestors were nearly twenty feet tall and could weigh more than seven tons. You're not sure what one of them could possibly be doing in this century, however.

Crabbe is as white as a sheet. "It has terrorized the locals for half a fortnight," he says. "You speak the monster's language, do you not? Parlay with it! Convince it to find its dinner elsewhere and leave us be!"

Toby, usually the quieter of the pair, has other ideas. "I say we gather an army and kill the serpent while it sleeps," he says. "We shall don flame-repellent clothing and rub ourselves with deadly nightshade, well known as the bane of all dragons. If we keep our wits, the beast will never stand a chance."

Okay, that guy's definitely going to get you killed. Still, it sounds like a better plan than facing the monster alone. Something weird is going on here, though. Maybe you should scout things out before committing to anything drastic.

▶ If you tell them you'll go alone, **turn to page 271.**

▶ *If you support Toby's plan—with some adjustments to focus more on gnashing teeth and less on magical fire—* **turn to page 41.**

Chance tromps off into the city, leaving you to your own devices. You get pretty bored, pretty fast. You examine the time-cycle, and although you can't figure out how it starts, you do find a secret compartment full of beef jerky. Which is nice, since the only thing you've had to eat since breakfast was that cookie.

You're still chewing when a jagged purple rift opens up in mid-air down the alleyway. Three gnarled little goblin creatures crawl out of it. One of them sees you and lets out a high-pitched squeal.

Suddenly, a column of light appears between you. A statu-esque mammal-woman in a silver jumpsuit steps out of it and smacks one of the goblins with a baton. The other two flee.

It's Velox of the Temporal Custodians. "We need your help," she says. "The interdimensional time goblins are mounting their final assault on our moonbase in 2271, and I'm gathering errant time travelers to join the fight."

"What about my partner, Chance? I'm supposed to guard his time machine."

She scoffs. "We have more than enough of those fools as it is. Leave the motorcycle. Or stay with it, if you prefer. I won't force you to come."

A final assault by interdimensional time goblins does sound important. Can you trust Velox, though? The last time you saw her you weren't exactly on the same page. Also, the two remaining goblins are peering at you from around a corner. If you leave the bike unguarded, you're sure they'll snatch it.

▶ *If you join Velox and head for the moon,* **turn to page 222.**

▶ *If you remain at your post and keep Chance's motorcycle from falling into the wrong hands,* **turn to page 154.**

You've witnessed the routine horrors inflicted upon the honest, hardworking serfdom of this era, and you'll be damned if you're going to let that injustice stand. That king is the most vile creature you've encountered anywhere in time, and his contemptible reign ends now.

Just as your resolve is all strengthened, you hear a scream from the other room. "Aaaaaaah! The child has murdered his highness!"

Apparently, Fleck is *way* ahead of you. "Kill the child! Kill the dog creature! Kill the Dragon Knight! KILL THEM AAAAAAALLLLLL!"

The guards who make up your escort may be uneasy around inexplicable magicks, but they didn't secure their cushy palace gig by panicking during assassination attempts. You feel their gauntlets tighten around you.

They stab you *a lot*.

THE END

You'll show *them* who shunts mutton! Granted, you have absolutely no combat training whatsoever, and there *are* twelve of them. Fortunately, Chance is a serious badass. The moment you make your move, he springs into action, launching into a fury of kicks and punches (you're pretty sure there's a backflip in there somewhere, too) and taking out nine of the thugs singlehandedly.

The other three run away.

"That was amazing!" you say as the last of his opponents falls to the ground, unconscious. "I was worried that your nod meant that you wanted to let them take us hostage."

"So they would take us to their boss!" Chance says. "That would have been a *much* better plan. Ah, well. Perhaps we can locate them with this." He pulls a device out of his satchel that looks like an old 1990s cell phone with a spinning disc attached to the end.

"It's a technolometer. Techno...*noligimer*?" His inability to pronounce the name of his own gadget doesn't inspire confidence. "Something like that. The little spinny thing detects any out-of-time technology within a three-mile radius. But I never find anything when I come to the 1880s. All of their metal limbs and robots and stuff are built with clockwork and steam power, nothing illegal. They're quite crafty, these ones."

Something is bugging you about the way Chance is holding the meter. "The spinning disc is the sensor?" you ask. "And it measures in a *radius*?"

"That's what they tell me. Why? Are there no radiuses here?"

You take the device from Chance and rotate it at a 90

(continue to the next page)

degree angle. It immediately starts beeping and showing two little green dots on its monochrome display.

"Brilliant!" Chance says. "It looks like there are two major violations. One is in the sky—in a blimp, no doubt. For some reason these people love blimps."

He takes back the doohickey and twists it around. "The other is deep in the earth below this building! Hmm… their underground complex will doubtlessly be well guarded. But how would we even get to the blimp? We could steal one of their hot air balloons, I suppose."

He seems unenthused with the idea. Then his gaze falls on the missile contraption abandoned by the ruffians. "Ooh! Do you think that thing might explode if we tried to ride it?"

Yes. Yes, you do. Chance is *clearly* insane. But if he's more worried about underground defenses than strapping himself to some random piece of artillery, how scary is the stuff *down there*?

▶ *If you try to commandeer a balloon and head blimpward,* **turn to page 67.**

▶ *If you'd rather keep to solid ground and investigate the underground bunker,* **turn to page 292.**

You decide to put your faith in the experienced time traveler (also, you're worried that if you disobey a direct order he might kick you). Your two alternate selves blast off on their rickety, steampunk rocket to wherever the hell they're going. Meanwhile, you and Chance spend about another half hour looking for his motorcycle before he gives it up as a lost cause and radios headquarters for a ride home.

He invites you back with him, and you accept, hoping to enlist the Time Patrol's help in your investigation. They eventually make you an officer, and you spend the next twenty years safeguarding the timestream (although not as Chance's partner—you ask to be reassigned when you discover that his office has an entire wall covered with portraits of former partners who met assorted grisly ends in the line of duty). You stop plenty of threats to the timeline during your time on the force, even if you never do run across the mad scientist you originally set out to look for. Heck, the story of how you lost an eye battling the robot spiders of 2077, alone, would make for an amazing book.

Alas, it isn't *this* one. The old, grizzled Time Patrol veteran version of you may still have a part to play in this adventure, but I'm afraid you'll have to read about it elsewhere.

THE END

Before you know it, you're back in Professor V.'s laboratory in 2271, still strapped into the time machine that Krikri modified to bypass the inherent limitations of Bakulan theory. The memories from your mammal-self are gone, but that's okay. Your dinosaur half was clearly the better of the two. Krikri is there as well, adjusting settings on the machine.

"Are you ready?" she asks. "I have no idea what these goblins truly are or what you might find in their heads. But I worry this might not be altogether... *safe*."

Okay, you *thought* you were ready, but now, she's starting to freak you out. "You'd better throw the switch," you say, "before I change my mind."

Soon your consciousness is back in the Cretaceous, drifting through the campsite just as a crack opens in reality and the first goblin skitters out of it. Up close the things look even more disturbing, with limbs contorted into impossible shapes, and skin that absorbs every iota of light unfortunate enough to strike it. For a moment you consider looking for the T. rex instead to see what three minds in the same body feels like. But you have a job to do. You sink into the goblin's head as it lurches across your path.

Inside, you find that the creature works on pure instinct, except for a tiny corner of its brain devoted to higher thought. As you access this portion, the goblin's twisted body suddenly splits down the middle, each half doubling its mass and sprouting the limbs lost in the process. Half of your consciousness goes with each, and the effect is disconcerting, to say the least.

You realize that the higher brains of both goblins are linked, and as more of the creatures emerge through the crevice, you

(continue to the next page)

discover that they share a rudimentary consciousness as well. It's a big, networked hivemind, and staring into it is like falling over a precipice into the abyss of madness.

It's all you can do to tear your mind away and return to the future before you lose your sanity completely. You take a jumbled collection of mental snapshots back with you and struggle to make sense of them as you describe your experience to Krikri. Seriously, it's *insane*. We're just going to give you the bullet points here because even *we* don't understand it a hundred percent.

• The interdimensional time goblins started out as the various duplicates of Hercule Von Krumpf in the Cretaceous until tachyon energy venting from an alternate version of their experiment in a nearby timeline completely collapsed their universe, trapping them in the space between realities.

• There, all possible versions of them existed simultaneously. The paradox of a conscious mind able to make decisions existing outside any universe that could be impacted by those decisions resulted in some pretty freaky temporal physics, creating the twisted, near-mindless creatures you encountered.

• Somehow, they managed to intentionally cause the very accident that spawned them in the first place. They traveled through vortexes in space-time and used technology they stumbled upon to send a comet on a collision course with Earth, altering the original Von Krumpf's timeline and forcing him to build his machine in an attempt to correct it.

Yeah, it doesn't make a ton of sense to us, either. There's something else, too. The prehistoric laser tower is only part of their plan. They're collecting the energy it emits and using it

(continue to the next page)

for some purpose elsewhere in time and space. Something… *apocalyptic*. The more you try to understand their plan, though, the more your brain refuses to comply. Your ranting grows less and less coherent, and Krikri tries in vain to calm you.

"It's okay!" she says. "You did it! Thanks to you, we have everything we need to set things right. Stay here and rest while I go back and tell the others. Don't worry, I'll return soon!"

In the blink of an eye, she's gone. No! You have to warn her about… *agh!* The corruption in your mind is growing like a cancer, and in your weakened state, you're powerless against it. You realize that this is the end. You have very little sanity left, and if you don't find a way to stave off the crazy, within moments your brain is going shut down completely.

The Bakulan device should still be dialed to the Cretaceous—if you re-merge your mind with the other version of you back there, will you be strong enough to fight off the madness? Or will you just damn the other version of yourself to insanity as well?

▶ *If you throw the switch, head back in time and hope for the best,* **turn to page 239.**

▶ *If you think it's too risky and remain in the future, leaving your primate-self to handle things from here,* **turn to page 72.**

"Townsfolk!" you say, pulling off your disguise. "This knight is my appointed champion. He has vanquished Lord Fenwick on the field of battle in my name! You owe him your allegiance!"

It works like a charm. The peasants lower their mud-farming implements and bow down. Before long, the bulk of the crowd has gone back to their homes, or mud fields, or wherever it is they go.

"I owe you a debt of gratitude, stranger," the dog knight says. "Or we're even, at the very least." He gives you a big Labrador smile. "I'm Boris. And you're of the Dinofolk, I presume?"

Of course—he's a fellow time traveler! Boris shows you his stopwatch, which turns out to be a time device similar to your armband but with one added feature: a circular screen in the center, which is currently displaying scenes from some kind of large-scale battle.

"When I first arrived this morning in your barn, my watch showed you battling Fenwick and losing." Boris says. "I hoped that taking your place and defeating him would set things right here, but that doesn't seem to be the case."

"Set things right?" you ask. "What do you mean?"

"When I fix the timeline, the light on top turns green, and I can go home." He pauses, and his eyes grow large. "Oh, no. I didn't accidentally kill the wrong guy, did I?"

"No," you insist. "That guy was a massive tool. Totally had it coming."

Boris looks relieved. You have no insight regarding local wrongs that may need righting, but he insists on finding the problem and repairing it to his watch's satisfaction, so you agree

(continue to the next page)

to help. He seems like a stand up guy (not to mention your best bet to catch a ride out of this hellhole). After a fair amount of legwork—the townsfolk now seem completely in awe of you but still have considerable difficulty answering simple questions—you determine that Lord Fenwick was in the service of a spectacularly awful king. By all accounts, he's cruel, vindictive, and at least borderline insane.

"That settles it, then," Boris says. "We arm the peasantry, mount a rebellion against this tyrant, win freedom for the townsfolk, and set up some sort of representative government." He checks his watch. "Shouldn't take more than a couple of days."

You feel a tug at your shirt. "Excuse me, your Gloriousnesses." It's Fleck, your friend from the barn. "I don't mean to speak out of turn, but if you wish to kill the king, why send us all to the battlefield? Why not simply sneak into the castle and be done with it?"

Boris seems affronted by the very idea. "Because that's not how things are done. You can't simply *give* people a revolution. It'll never stick. If they want their freedom, they must rise up and seize it!"

Fleck scrunches up her little face and shrugs. "Our lives aren't worth much out here in the mud, but even so, thousands of them in barter for one king seems a lot to ask."

▶ *If you agree with Boris and think an honest revolution is the way to go,* **turn to page 287.**

▶ *If you like the sound of Fleck's assassination idea,* **turn to page 204.**

You are not a prehistoric monster! YOU ARE A HUMAN BEING! You swallow the last of the Edmontosaurus entrails (delicious, delicious Edmontosaurus entrails) and focus on the things that tie you to the civilized world. Cherished childhood memories. Your loved ones. That really good first season of *Downton Abbey*. Slowly, the ravenous carnosaur subsides and you feel your humanity bubbling to the surface.

Suddenly, a colossal shape thunders toward you. A second tyrannosaur has apparently caught wind of your kill and decided to challenge you for the carcass. It's bigger than you, looks *a lot* meaner, and lets out a ferocious howl that tells you it senses weakness.

How's that humanity working out for you?

▶ *Never mind! If you let the prehistoric monster back out,* **turn to page 58.**

▶ *No! Your humanity is all you have! If you attempt to SMART your way out of this,* **turn to page 74.**

"Oh my God, *so* amazing," you say. "The impressions were so... *vague*. But in a good way? And the image snippets! I mean... wow. Just *wow*."

You worry that you may be laying it on a bit thick, but she's right there with you. "I *know*, right?" She pauses, awkwardly shaking your little hand. "They call me Velox, by the way. Welcome to the lunar command center of the Temporal Custodians."

She proceeds to give you the royal tour. You discover that most of the base is covered in glass (or some similarly transparent material) offering breathtaking views of the surrounding moonscape. The bright, daytime sky is filled with spinning, disk-shaped aircraft, buzzing all over the place.

Now *that's* the kind of thing you traveled to the distant future to see. "So many ships," you say. "Where are they all going?"

"Ships?" Velox cocks an eyebrow. "Some visitors report seeing various phenomena in the skies here, but they're just illusions that plague lesser minds in close proximity to the Great Consciousness." She looks at you suspiciously. "I'm sure the visions will clear up as you get your bearings." As she speaks, one of the ships approaches, hovering above the glass ceiling just behind her.

A green-skinned man in a jumpsuit matching Velox's stops in the hallway, waiting patiently for her to finish her conversation. Then, a column of red light erupts from the spacecraft above, completely disintegrating him the spot.

Velox turns abruptly at the sound of his brief, terrified scream. "Control!" she says, tapping a communications device

(continue to the next page)

hidden in her ear. "Did the Great Consciousness send Cadet Flppto on a time jump just now?"

Great Consciousness? "You SERIOUSLY didn't see that ship?" you ask, your voice betraying a bit more panic than you'd prefer.

"Enough with the ships!" Velox snaps. Apparently she's not pleased with whatever response she received. "We have to get to the jump room. Hurry!"

The UFOs outside seem to have launched a full-scale attack, and you have to dive out of the way more than once to avoid being caught in their beams. Nevertheless, jumpsuited mammalfolk continue about their business calmly, occasionally stopping in bewildered silence if a coworker happens to disintegrate right before their eyes.

You finally arrive at a large, domed room. "I'm afraid I must ask you to undertake your first mission as a Temporal Custodian rather abruptly," Velox says. "This is Krikri, one of our top agents."

She introduces you to the dolphin-headed woman you met back in Professor V.'s lab. "It's a pleasure to meet you," Krikri says. If she recognizes you, she shows no sign of it. How many talking dinosaurs does she hang around with? Of course, when you first encountered her, you were the one standing there looking confused. You realize that the intricacies of working with other time travelers is going to take some getting used to.

"I'm sending the two of you to investigate these mysterious disappearances," Velox says. "If you trust the Great Consciousness, it will always send you where you need to be. So whatever era you find yourself in, take careful notes and report

(continue to the next page)

back promptly."

Your eyes are locked on one of the alien crafts, floating above the domed ceiling. "Velox, we're being attacked!" you say. "I know you think I'm hallucinating, but I swear to you, every single one of your 'mysterious disappearances' has been accompanied by a friggin' UFO and a terrifying column of fire!"

Velox just frowns. Krikri catches your eye and gives you a quick head-shake.

"There's one right there!" you insist, pointing at the hovering ship. Just then, a beam of light erupts into the room, just a few feet from where you're standing.

Krikri looks at you, then glances at the red light and jerks her neck, gesturing toward it with her big dolphin nose. What does she want you to do? Push Velox into it? Whatever's going on here, you don't think murder is the answer.

Velox, of course, ignores the beam completely. "Time jump will initiate in five… four… three… two…"

Before Velox reaches zero, Krikri leaps into the column and vanishes. WHAT. THE. HELL. The Great Consciousness of the Persistent Universe *did* tell you to trust her. Then again, you're fairly sure that thing's nuts. Whatever you're going to do, though, you have roughly a second and a half to decide.

▶ *If you hurl yourself into the column of light—which may or may not have just completely disintegrated Krikri—* **turn to page 240.**

▶ *If you stand still and let Velox time-jump you instead,* **turn to page 53.**

"So long, sucker!" You sprint across the room, dart past the robot, and chuck yourself into the open tube.

You've seen enough movies to know how this works! The garbage chute will lead to a trash compactor level (possibly with an unexplained tentacle monster that somehow makes its home there), and you'll make your last-minute escape as soon as the walls start to compress, threatening to squash you like a bug. Of course, you don't have a trusty droid companion to shut down the garbage smashers for you, so that could be an issue. Maybe that worker robot can lend a hand. It looked almost as sick of hearing about the magical, all-knowing Persistent Universe as you are.

Alas, after a brief period of freefall, the first thing you learn is that as advanced as these people seem to be, they don't find it necessary to make their garbage any more compact before dumping it off base. The second thing you learn is that this particular base is on the surface of the moon.

Fun fact! Did you know that temperatures on the moon's surface can reach upward of 250 degrees fahrenheit on the side exposed to direct sunlight?

You start to burn up as you suffocate to death but happily lose consciousness almost immediately, so are spared the really nasty part.

THE END

DAMMIT, VON KRUMPF. If you knew he was going to pull this crap, you would have just let the bloody *robot* dinosaur destroy his stupid laser beam. It looks like it's up to you, though. You charge the tower at ramming speed, hoping that your tyrannosaur bulk is enough to topple it, or at least knock it out of alignment or something and thwart his villainous plan.

Instead, you barely even touch the supercharged outer structure, and all seven tons of you burn to a crisp like a moth in a bug zapper.

Fortunately, Von Krumpf was on the up and up after all. The tower momentarily powers down on its own, and Krikri, Professor Venkataraman, Bruxelles, and a few goblins who haven't quite managed to get themselves into dimensional rifts are treated to a heartwarming reunion between Hercule and the love of his life, who he's literally torn the fabric of space and time asunder to find.

Seriously, you should learn to be more trusting.

The End

The cookie thing is an exercise meant to show the ramifications of free will, but the truth is that, in this particular instance, Professor V. is just going to give you the rest of the lecture regardless of which cookie you pick.

Sorry for the letdown.

▶ Turn to page 282.

Oh, hello giant spaceship full of terrifying interdimensional time goblins. I brought you this handheld nuclear weapon.

SUCK ON IT.

You detonate the device, which blows the hell out of the mothership's inner workings, sending it careening down to the moon below. The blast doesn't have any measurable effect on the rift in space-time, which remains floating in the empty space the ship leaves behind, but it does kill a large portion of the goblin horde.

And you, of course. It kills the *hell* out of you. But destroying the ship disables the shield protecting their stronghold on the abandoned Temporal Custodian base, meaning that your noble sacrifice gives the rest of the assembled forces the chance they need to stop the goblins' evil plot once and for all. You die a hero.

A really, *really* vaporized hero.

The End

"The Reverse Engineer is the finest mind we've ever recruited," Beatrice says. "Even the other gizmologists will tell you that. He's the one who finds ways to reconstruct future technologies using 1880s materials, which keeps that contemptible Time Patrol at bay."

She takes you down a big, fancy elevator to a thoroughly modern underground laboratory and introduces you to two men. "This is our roboticist, Mr. Saito, and our chronologist, Mr. Venkataraman. But gentlemen! Wherever is Mr. Von Krumpf?"

Saito just harrumphs and turns back to his computer terminal. His colleague, however, takes one look at you and bolts for the back door. It's Bobbins from the Gas Can Rebellion! Or some alternate version of him, perhaps—he looks a smidge heavier and has added a goatee to his meticulously trimmed facial hair.

"Oh my, he's certainly on edge," Beatrice says. "Mr. Venkataraman is from just a few years in the future, where his wife and son were tragically killed by a runaway automaton or some such thing."

She explains that he found his way through a time portal and now is willing to do just about anything for them if they promise to keep his future wife and unborn child safe. "It's quite remarkable," she says. "We keep thinking we'll find his ethical limit, but he certainly hasn't reached it yet. Mr. Von Krumpf thinks his child must be destined to build a time machine, since the universe is working so diligently to keep him in the timestream."

The elevator dings, and you turn to see a group of thugs wheel in a futuristic motorcycle. "You fools!" Beatrice says.

(continue to the next page)

"You stole one of their vehicles? This will bring the Time Patrol to our doorstep for certain!"

"Reverse Engineer's orders, boss," one of them says. "Offered five dollars to anyone who could bring him a timecycle."

"And five dollars you'll get!" You recognize the voice, as well as the ragged beard and wild-eyed expression that go with it. The dapper coat and hat are new, but the man who comes barging into the room is definitely the same mad scientist you encountered in 1983.

"Do you understand what this means?" he howls. "The timecycle is shielded! I can use its parts to keep the goblins out of the portals! FIVE DOLLARS FOR EVERYONE!"

Beatrice is fuming. "Damn it, Von Krumpf, the goblins are *not your concern*. That contraption is useless! We've never been able to circumvent Time Patrol security measures."

When the scientist sees you, his face breaks out in a huge, unsettling smile. "If it's an unshielded portal you want, use the dinosaur's device. Those first generation armbands don't have any security measures whatsoever."

The room falls silent, and all eyes turn to you. Uh oh. Have the sisters only been keeping you alive because they assume they can't use your time travel technology without your permission? You make a mental note to ask Professor Velociraptor to add some security measures the next time you see her.

"What? No, this is a *third* generation armband! *So* secure! You can't use it without, like, *all these secret codes*—"

You get shot seven times before you can even finish babbling.

The End

The landing isn't pretty, and it wrecks what's left of your ship, but at least you walk away from it. The moonbase is abandoned and in frightful condition. Doors are bashed in, shattered glass is everywhere, and scorch marks decorate the walls. It has power—and life support, which you probably should have checked before you left the ship—but Krikri checks the logs and can find no record of what happened.

"I'm going to travel back and investigate," she says. "I'll bring you a working time device if I can find one." With a blip, she's gone, and you settle in for what could be a *really* long stay.

You start poking around in the custodians' files and find entire libraries worth of scientific texts. You could spend a lifetime studying time travel in this place. Or space travel, for that matter. Hmm… either of those pursuits could eventually lead to a ticket out of here.

As you're pondering your options, Krikri reappears. Rather than bringing you a working time machine, though, she wants to borrow your broken one.

"I think Professor Venkataraman can help me fix it, then Professor Vegetatious can shield it, so the goblins can't attack us midstream. It's kind of a lot to explain. But if all goes well, I'll return with it when I'm done."

You can't help wondering what happens to you on the moon if all *doesn't* go well. Studying time travel is a bit pointless if you don't have a time machine to repair. Of course, you could always commit to fixing the spacecraft instead.

▶ *If you give Krikri the armband,* **turn to page 47.**

▶ *If you tell her you need it,* **turn to page 248.**

You know, Chance isn't the one with his freaking *mouth* tied shut. If he wants you to go peacefully with the people who have just been ordered to murder you, he can damn well say something out loud next time. Your razor-sharp teeth may be off the table, but you've got other tricks up your sleeve. You launch into a spin-attack, knocking both of the thugs behind you down with your tail—

And immediately feel a powerful jolt of electricity and the complete loss of muscle control. Hey! Nobody told you these guys had *tasers*. Your brief hope that your partner will save you is dashed when you see him hit the floor and twitch helplessly beside you.

Then the hail of bullets starts. You're dead before the time-shifted, alternate versions of you and Chance waiting outside can even *try* to rescue you.

THE END

You can do this, right? I mean, Krikri is the kindest, most gentle soul you've encountered in any millennium, and *she* apparently killed an alternate dolphin lady to peel herself from the space-time continuum.

You hop into the swirling vortex and emerge right behind the other you, staring at the two portals. This must be just *seconds* ago. Without giving yourself a chance to reconsider, you descend upon your double in a fury of gnashing teeth. The other dinosaur has apparently come to the same conclusion you have about doing what needs to be done, because it doesn't put up any kind of fight whatsoever.

Somehow that only makes it *worse.*

It's over in moments, and you shrug off the gut-wrenching sensation of being torn from the fabric of the universe. You haven't got time for existential angst. Around you, the tachyon shield sputters back to life. You did it! Well, technically Professor Venkataraman did it, but you *helped*! There are still quite a few goblins inside the barrier, but at least you've staved off the deluge.

The first portal closes, but before the second one does, a huge mass of gleaming steel comes crashing through it, sending hunks of soil flying as it skids across the ground. It springs to its feet and emits a piercing, mechanical screech.

Staring at you with glowing red eyes is a robotic Tyrannosaurus rex, every inch as large as you and somehow twice as fearsome.

First of all, WHAT THE HELL? Professor V.'s idea of escaping to safety is the *land of robot freaking dinosaurs*? Second of all, savage prehistoric beast or no, it's obvious that this thing

(continue to the next page)

has you vastly outmatched. It moves with terrifying grace, outweighs you by a factor of five, and its metal hide renders your teeth useless. You're fairly certain it could kill you ten times over before you could even dent it.

You hear a snap, and the bottom half of Krikri's stick weapon skitters across the ground at your feet. To your left, you see a dozen goblins pile on top of her. Ahead, the mecha-tyrannosaur launches itself toward the tower. And the only thing in its path with even the slightest chance of slowing it down is *you*.

▶ *If you rush to Krikri's aid,* **turn to page 56.**

▶ *If you hurl yourself at your robotic counterpart and defend the tower at any cost,* **turn to page 272.**

You pull that son of a bitch. A shower of sparks flies from the switchbox, and the cabin goes dark, which you take to be a good sign. But then you hear a low thrumming sound, followed by an intense flash of light. You glance up and see that the orb is growing in both size and luminescence. It's also pulsing and shimmering, like a big, scary disco ball of doom.

Uh oh.

The guards stop firing and start fleeing the cabin like rats on a sinking ship. You rush to Annie and try to revive her, but she's out cold. Crap. Dragging her off this boat with your tiny dinosaur arms is going to be a *major* pain in the ass. Fortunately, Cartwright comes to your aid. Her right arm is soaked in blood and hanging limp at her side, but she hoists Annie with her left.

"To the hangar!" she says. "Hurry!" You follow her to the spot where you left your vehicles and find Pippa and Skip prepping them for takeoff. Without missing a beat, Cartwright leaps onto one of the contraptions and pushes herself out the open hatch. You quickly follow suit with both Powder Monkeys in tow.

The trip back is roughly eighty times more terrifying than your initial voyage was, but you manage to land your craft in one piece. Cartwright is there already, sprawled out on the cobblestone street and cradling Annie in her lap.

"Her battery," Cartwright says, her face streaked with tears. "It's shot. When she got hit with that shock rod…" She trails off.

If it's power she needs, you've got that covered. Cartwright rips open the laces on Annie's corset to reveal a mess of gears and copper tubing along with a power port identical to the ones on the ornithoptivelocipede engines. You rush to your friend's side…

(continue to the next page)

And discover that your time travel bracelet is missing from your wrist.

Missing? Or *never there to begin with*? Although you're now immune to the ravages of temporal causality, the same can't be said for your *stuff*. Your memories of the recent past remain intact, but somehow, the images of Professor Velociraptor within them are becoming... *fuzzy*. Could something that happened here in the 1880s *erase* the professor from the timestream?

With Annie lying unconscious, there's no time to unravel that particular tangle of paradoxes.

You're not sure if invisible, magic gas operates on the same basic principles as a car battery, but it's worth a shot. You and Cartwright heave Annie over to one of the vehicles, line up their respective ports, wrap the copper pipes together with cloth torn from your coat, and rev the engine.

Annie awakens with a gasp. "What the HELL just happened?" It's not pretty, but your jury-rigged jumpstart is enough to keep her gears turning until she can make the necessary repairs.

As for the airship, a follow-up recon mission uncovers no sign of it. Whatever the sisters' plan was, it seems to have either yanked them out of this reality altogether or gone horribly wrong and burned them to a crisp. Their automaton army remains, though, and one of their lackeys steps in to fill the power vacuum they leave behind. The Gas Can Rebellion has its work cut out for it.

You spend the rest of your days fighting the good fight alongside them.

THE END

Seriously, how are *you* supposed to know which bomb to use? For just a moment you ponder the utter unjustness of being presented with a potentially life-or-death decision while having very little in the way of relevant information. Then you take a stab in the dark.

"DISRUPTOR!" you yell back to your passenger.

It works remarkably well. The child heaves something heavy-looking that's approximately the size of his head into the hatch, and you're treated to a loud zap and a burst of electricity arcing momentarily from the hole. Some kind of automated gun turret descends limply from the ship's undercarriage but just hangs there, motionless. Since you're already on a direct course, you go ahead and fly straight into the open portal. Inside, you find a scattering of clockwork centurions, all deactivated by the bomb. Meanwhile, Annie and Bobbins have been similarly successful in their own aerial adventures and join you in the launch bay presently. "Good show, everyone," Annie says. "Now, I do believe we have an evil plot to thwart."

A little recon reveals an enormous central chamber swarming with thugs and automatons beneath a glowing, translucent orb that hangs from the ceiling. A pair of men you don't recognize are working at two separate terminals, but the sisters are nowhere to be seen.

"My God," Annie says, pointing a device she calls a sensitrometer at the orb. "It's drawing power from the airship's engines, but also... *somewhere else.* It's charging rapidly, too— the power levels are increasing exponentially. Whatever it's doing, it's doing it *soon.*"

She smiles. "Fortunately, I have a plan. I'll get to the control

(continue to the next page)

panel on the far side of the room and reroute power, so any attempt to turn that thing on will just fry the engines. A ship this unwieldy can't possibly fly without power, so that should be the end of it. Pippa, Skip, you take your bag of tricks and start spreading bombs around. They've built this vessel to resist explosives, but if my plan doesn't work, we might still take her down the old fashioned way."

The Powder Monkeys nod and take off running. "Bobbins," Annie continues, "do you see that big switch? That'll be the device's trigger. Stay hidden, then get to it and flip it the moment I give you the signal."

"You make it sound rather easy," Bobbins says. "What should I do if one of these robots or ruffians interferes?"

Annie turns to you and Cartwright. "That's where the two of you come in. I need one of you to create a distraction and draw their fire while the other one takes out as many guards as possible. You can start with those two stationed in the rafters." She points to a pair of goons with ornate, scoped energy rifles monitoring the room from above.

Cartwright gives you a nervous look. "Distraction duty's a suicide mission," she says, holding out a gun that's similar to the one the thugs have, only bigger. "I'll do it. You take care of those snipers."

Since you've never fired a weapon in your life, sharp-shooting isn't exactly your area of expertise. But what's the alternative? Running into the room waving your hands, trying to encourage a few dozen soldiers to shoot at *you*?

▶ *If you take the gun,* **turn to page 44.**

▶ *If you let Cartwright keep it, volunteering for the decoy/ suicide job yourself,* **turn to page 262.**

You let your consciousness seep into the Labrador, surprised at how much it feels like home. Alas, spying on the scientist proves painfully dull: he essentially runs around the house in a constant state of agitation, working out complex mathematical equations and accusing his pet of espionage.

Which, you now realize, is pretty much accurate.

Over the next few days, you and Krikri take turns going further and further back, piecing together the scientist's history. Saddled with the unfortunate name Hercule Von Krumpf, he was just ten in 1941 when the U.S. joined the war against Germany, and suddenly his classmates found the moniker not just silly but also sinister. He was clearly a brilliant child, though his intellect rarely translated into academic achievement. He finished high school but barely made it through a single semester of college before dropping out. The following five years were spent working a string of low-paying jobs and immersing himself in his private studies.

Then in 1955, alone in his garage, he invented the Bakulan method of time travel.

"We always thought the invention was in '31 because that's as far back as we could travel," you tell Krikri. "But that's the year the inventor of time travel was *born*. The whole science of Bakulan time travel—it's all centered around this one guy."

"Which means he invented time travel *twice*," Krikri says. "Bakulan in 1955, then non-Bakulan in 1983." Her little dolphin eyes widen. "The tachyon particles must bounce off him like *crazy*."

You continue your observations but don't find much to further your understanding of Von Krumpf's motivation.

(continue to the next page)

Because he could never travel before the year of his own birth, his machine only allowed him to inhabit his own body and relive various moments in a life that was filled with loneliness and disappointment. He used the device less and less frequently over the years and never shared his invention with another soul, living in increasing seclusion. Finally, in 1983, he seemed to go completely over the deep end for no reason you can determine and started working frantically on the second machine.

Krikri has a theory about it. "With this machine, we can only see events that happen in one specific timeline," she says. "But I think something happened in '83 that altered that timeline. And because he's a time travel inventor, his memories didn't completely change with it. That would explain why he snapped, and his renewed interest in time travel."

She thinks she can use her own technology, along with the data stored in the TTIA computers, to develop a merged form of time travel that will allow you to send your consciousness into alternate timelines and test her hypothesis. However, you're starting to become less interested in 1983 and more worried about 2271. You still haven't uncovered evidence of other people living anywhere on Earth, and the various canisters of weird future-food you found in the employee break room are all but gone.

Physically, you're still stuck here. Perhaps, it's time to turn your attention to the present?

▶ *If you support Krikri's plan to continue research into the past,* **turn to page 274.**

▶ *If you'd rather focus on the very real concerns of the present,* **turn to page 26.**

Betsy hates bath time *a lot*, so the muscle memory is all there. You clamp down on that sumbitch's arm with your teeth and thrash around like mad until you free yourself, knocking your captor half off his feet in the process. He stumbles forward trying to regain balance, tumbles head first into the pulsing blue beam, and is instantly disintegrated.

See? *That's* why you thought this whole thing was a bad idea to begin with.

One of the other clones, manning a station at a nearby console, drops to his knees. "It worked!" he exclaims. "One second I was falling into the beam, and the next second… My God, I have both sets of memories. But my head feels… *clearer.*" Apparently this particular duplicate is the ideal mad scientist of all possible universes. With the sheer volume of them on hand, you suppose it makes sense one of them would be.

(continue to the next page)

"You can't be the prime!" Longbeard sputters. "*I'm* the prime! None of you spent years trapped in the Middle Ages! None of you solved the shielding problem in 1882! It *has* to be me!"

The merged clone starts pacing back and forth, shaking his head. "It doesn't matter who the prime is," he says. "What we're doing here—it's all wrong. I can't... I can't figure out why, but it's broken."

"No! We're getting him back! I won't let you stop me!" Longbeard pulls a gun from under his coat. It's the same one he used to shoot his alternate self back in the 1980s, and judging by his clenched teeth, he means to use it.

Should you intervene? The newly fused double-doppelganger seems by far the most reasonable of the lot, and might just be the key to ending all this madness. Then again, you're one dog. What can you hope to accomplish here, other than getting yourself shot?

▶ *If you throw yourself at Longbeard and try to snatch the gun out of his hand,* **turn to page 137.**

▶ *If you decide not to get involved and just sneak away during the commotion,* **turn to page 40.**

Of course you're going to pick the dino-timeline. Before this week, you didn't even know there *were* any others. And because it's the timeline that created you, it literally includes every single person you've ever met (at least until all this chrono-nonsense got started). What other decision could you have made?

The fact that you can't be certain that *you* exist in either of the other universes, of course, didn't enter into your decision at all.

After a brief moment of confusion and vertigo that feels like an uncomfortably tight hug from every single molecule that will ever exist in any universe, you open your eyes to see the gentle expression of Professor Velociraptor. You're back in the Time Travel Investigation Agency, and she's unstrapping you from the Bakulan time travel machine.

You start to tell her what you've just gone through—she has a secret back room with fancy time travel armbands, so she'll understand, right?—but stop yourself. You're still peeled off of the space-time continuum, and this is the universe that made you. If you keep messing with time travel, will you just start screwing that up again? Since this is the sole existing timeline, is non-Bakulan time travel even still *possible*? And if it is, do you want anything to do with it? Or would you rather just quit this godforsaken business and go find a job that doesn't involve messing with the very fabric of the freaking universe? Like, you don't know, *retail* or something?

Take some time to decide. If nothing else, you've earned a break.

THE END

You swore an oath to the Time Patrol—multiple oaths! in triplicate!—and you take your duty to protect the timestream seriously. Besides, whatever's going on here in 1882 is *messed up*. You're one hundred percent committed to the mission at hand.

Of course, that mission is already doomed to complete and utter failure, but that doesn't make your dedication to it any less noble.

The thing is, stuff's going down on that airship *right now*, and there's a zero percent chance your pokey little balloon can get you there in time to stop it. After what seems like an eternity, you rise above the cloud cover and see an enormous dirigible glowing like a beacon in the moonlight.

It promptly explodes, killing you instantly.

THE END

The Persistent Universe—whatever that thing was—told you to put your trust in Krikri, and so far, she hasn't given you any reason to doubt those instructions. You tell her to hunt down Von Krumpf and report back as soon as she discovers where the portal went back in 1983.

She blips out of existence for a fraction of a second, then reappears in exactly the same spot. "Found him!" she exclaims. Wow, that was fast. Then you realize that, regardless of how long her search was, of course she'd come back at the same moment she left. For all you know, she could have spent weeks—or even years—searching.

Time travel is weird.

It turns out Von Krumpf traveled to the late Cretaceous Period, which makes sense if he was hoping to either cause or prevent the extinction of the dinosaurs. Krikri plugs the exact moment of his arrival into the upgraded time machine—she insists that it will have no trouble sending you to a time prior to 1931, since breaking those rules was the whole point of cross-Bakulation—and soon, your consciousness is making one last trip to the distant past.

When you arrive, you find yourself floating above some kind of savage junglescape. In a clearing beneath you is Von Krumpf, currently attempting to flee the scene through a time portal. He's immediately blocked by Krikri, who pops through the portal from the other side. Also present is a giant, prehistoric ancestor of modern tyrannoids, roaring in fury.

Looks like you've just found your Cretaceous host body.

You settle into the dinosaur's brain but are surprised to find another foreign entity already in there. From what you can

(continue to the next page)

sense, it's some type of mammal-person—the scientist, perhaps? No, that wouldn't make sense. Whoever it is, though, it's having a hell of a time trying to control the tyrannosaur, and the battle of wills is apparently the source of the animal's anger. Well, that and the fact that it hasn't had anything to eat all day.

Even after millions of years of evolution, you share quite a bit of DNA with this dinosaur and shouldn't have much trouble calming it down and using it as a host. You're more worried about the mammal consciousness, though.

Hmm. Krikri's right there. Maybe you should just abandon the whole dinosaur idea and park yourself in her head instead, at least until you can come up with a better plan.

▶ *If you focus on taming the primal fury of the T. rex,* **turn to page 254.**

▶ *If you choose Krikri as your host instead,* **turn to page 155.**

Two huge, razor-toothed dinosaur heads are better than one, right? There are crates scattered along the chamber's walls, and you sneak to the closest one, stopping for a brief rest behind it. The distance to the next crate is short, so you wait for a pair of guards to pass by, then scoot over to it. This is going well! As long as the other you stays hidden in that room, you should make it there in no time.

The other you, however, has *very* different ideas about how to handle a small army of robots and thugs. Just as you're halfway to your next hiding spot, your double leaps out into the chamber, screaming. Most of the thugs react to a roaring dinosaur surprise by freaking the hell out and running in the opposite direction. Which is, unfortunately, more or less toward you. The first one to see you screams "lizard monster!" and faints dead away.

The next few, however, are made of sterner stuff. They regain their composure long enough to draw weapons and fire on this second monster, which is staring at them, motionless, like a deer in the headlights.

Basically, the other version of yourself promptly gets you killed. *Goddamnit, alternate universe doppelganger.*

THE END

You clamp down on the king's head with your enormous maw and rip it right off his shoulders, crown and all. It's by far the most disgusting thing you've ever done.

At this point, several things happen at once. First, Boris sees the light on the top of his stopwatch turn green and disappears with a flash of light and a triumphant "woohoo." Second, Fleck ducks away to safety beneath the legs of the king's guards. And third, you're hit from behind by an axe, the blades of several swords, and at least a dozen crossbow bolts.

You are well and truly dead before you even know what hit you.

As far as the local peasantry, we're happy to report that life is significantly improved under the king's half-brother, Albert the Significantly Less Inbred. He proves a benevolent and thoughtful ruler and takes a particular interest in Fleck after interviewing her about the assassination incident. He invites her entire family to live and work at the royal castle although he has no better success in determining her physical gender than you did.

In fact, rather than subjecting himself to an awkward conversation after it's WAY too late to simply ask, King Albert decrees that the populace adopt a gender-neutral pronoun, and by the time the 20th century rolls around, the word "thon" is in common usage as a way to say "he" or "she" without specifying male or female. Wait—could the tyranny of *gendered pronouns* have been the injustice Boris was sent back in time to correct *all along*?

YOU DECIDE.

THE END

The Time Patrol sounds like the exact opposite of the Time Travel Investigation Agency that has employed you for the past six months. Which is to say: *awesome.*

"Sign me up," you say.

Captain Steele insists that you hand over your armband—apparently, non-authorized time travel devices can cause problems with their systems, and she can't take the risk. After a surprising amount of paperwork—you do have to literally sign up on like 14 different forms, all of them in triplicate—you're ready to begin your first-day orientation. Chance brings you to a building marked "Experimental Weaponry" and introduces you to a smallish woman in a lab coat.

"Professor V.!" he says, beaming. "Looking good, as always! And human today, be still my heart."

The woman looks more or less like all the other mammal-people you've met today although, so far, she's the only one with streaks of gray in her hair. Something in her eyes, however, looks strikingly familiar. Could this really be the same Professor V. you know from the dino-timeline?

"Officer Bruxelles," she says. "Always the charmer." She turns to you, glances at your tiny arms, rethinks the handshake and gives you a little pat on the shoulder.

"This must be our new recruit," she says. "I'm Professor Venkataraman, Chief Technology Officer for Time Patrol. I'm also the only one in this base who isn't peeled off of the space-time continuum, so the first thing you'll have to get used to is the fact that as things change throughout the multiverse, my appearance may alter... *dramatically.*"

Well, that's kind of fun. "As a Time Patrol Officer," she

(continue to the next page)

continues, "there's one rule you must always observe. It is absolutely vital that you never, *under any circumstances*, bring a visitor to Time Patrol HQ who isn't peeled off from space-time. I'm a time machine inventor, so special rules apply to me. But any other causality-dependent individual in this pocket of sideways-space could tear a hole in our shielding. The results would be catastrophic."

"Yes, yes," Chance says. "Never bring anyone who isn't peeled off, yadda yadda. Now do the cookie thing!"

"What's the cookie thing?" you ask.

Professor V. sighs. "It illustrates an age-old question that people have pondered for centuries," she says. "What makes us human? What separates a conscious being from an unthinking animal? A religious person might call it a soul, but I prefer to think of it as the definition of 'sentience.' And the answer is no less than the ability to cause a rift in the universe and split the very fabric of space-time."

She holds out a small plate with two cookies on it. One of them is chocolate with additional chunks of semi-sweet chocolate baked into it. The other looks like it's probably oatmeal. It has raisins.

"Choose one," Professor V. says.

▶ *If you choose the oatmeal raisin cookie,*
   turn to page 176.

▶ *If you choose the chocolate chocolate chunk,*
   turn to page 282.

You are not an animal! YOU ARE A HUMAN BEING! And more importantly, you're a junior agent of the Time Travel Investigation Agency. Every minute of your training has prepared you for… hmm. Actually, your training assured you that today's events were utterly impossible and you'd never have to deal with anything remotely like them. Nevertheless, there's a madman loose in the corridors of time, and you appear to be the only one who can stop him.

You sample the air with your enormous T. rex nasal cavities and are treated to a panoramic wonderland of aromas. As your brain acclimates to your powerful new sniffer, you manage to pick out the distinctive scent of cigarette smoke mixed with Aqua Velva. That's a 1980s mad scientist if you've ever smelled one!

You follow the trail upwind and discover your quarry crouched in a patch of shrubbery, scavenging for berries. The thought of eating makes hunger pangs in your belly rumble anew, but there will be plenty of time to satisfy your cravings once you've thwarted this villain's evil—

Hold the phone. Put those two ideas together and you just might be in business.

▶ *If you straight up eat that son of a bitch,*
  turn to page 265.

▶ *If you get ahold of yourself and try to subdue him in a less lethal manner,* **turn to page 78.**

You head for the commotion in the foliage and IMMEDIATELY REGRET YOUR DECISION. Sure enough, a pack of smallish velociraptor-looking things (technically they're "bambiraptors," which makes all of this that much more humiliating) is disembowelling a large herbivore, but the moment they see you lumbering across their path, they abandon their meal in favor of a fresh kill.

A few of the scientists behind you also fall prey to their piranha-like appetite, but those guys are pretty much a renewable resource at this point. There's only one Betsy and only one investigator camped out inside her. And before you know it, you're—OH GOD, THE CARNAGE! THEY'RE TEARING YOU LIMB FROM LIMB AND FEASTING ON YOUR INTESTINES, BUT YOU'RE STILL ALIVE AND CAN FEEL EVERY—AAAAAAAAAAAAAGH! WHY DIDN'T YOU CHOOSE THE FOREBODING TEMPORAL RIFT? WHYYYYYYYYYYYYYYYY...?

THE END

Once again, the universe dissolves under your feet. Now, you seem to be a cross between a normal monkey-person and some kind of... *Lord of the Rings* creature? Slowly, your head clears. You're a half-orc. And you're riding a horse-drawn carriage with your two companions, a bearded, axe-wielding dwarf and a gnome tinkerer. What's so weird about that?

Everything, a tiny voice says inside your head. Reality is shifting around you, and the reason you're not perfectly in sync with the shifts isn't just due to tachyon particulate. It's because a version of you from a different timeline merged its mind with yours at some point, and some remnant of it remains.

Some small part of your consciousness is peeled off of the space-time continuum.

For the moment, however, you have more pressing concerns. Your carriage is barreling over a long, wooden bridge, and an army of—some kind of evil minion or another, it's difficult to make them out clearly at this speed—is following close behind.

"They're gaining on us!" the dwarf says. "We have to blow the bridge!"

"If we do, the townsfolk will be cut off from their supply line!" the gnome says. "And we'll *never* get paid!"

"If we don't blow it, we'll be *dead*!" the dwarf fires back.

"If we do blow it, we'll be *poor*!"

▶ *If you blow the bridge,* **turn to page 35.**

▶ *If you leave it intact and try to find another way to escape your pursuers,* **turn to page 286.**

The first order of business is to decide what to call you, since your new friends agree that your given name won't do at all. After considerable debate they settle on "Thunder Lizard." The second order of business is to devise a plan.

Annie is in favor of using you to gather intel. "To the sisters, you're still a wild card," she says. "We can send you into their lair, and if they think you can offer them something, they'll tell us everything we need to know. Say we brought you to our hideout after the gang busted me out of jail, and you have information to trade. It's the perfect plan."

"Perfect if you want to tip our hand, you mean," Cartwright says. "We've got the power source. I say we saddle up for an all-out assault on their compound, and do it fast before they suspect anything."

Annie puts the matter to a vote, and Bobbins sides with her while the Powder Monkeys prefer Cartwright's plan. "That's three to two," Cartwright says.

"You know full well the little'uns only get one vote between them," Annie fires back. "It's two to two, even split. Looks like our new recruit will have to break the tie."

Hmmm. You don't relish the idea of embarking on a spy mission without any backup, but going in with guns blazing sounds absurdly dangerous as well. You start doing the math, trying to decide which plan is least likely to result in your untimely death.

▶ *If you volunteer for the spy mission,* **turn to page 115.**

▶ *If you were sold on the second choice the moment we used the phrase "guns blazing,"* **turn to page 246.**

It takes some work to convince Boris that skullduggery is the best course of action, but after a short while, the images on his timepiece change to show an old, confused-looking man on a golden throne, and that seals the deal. Now, you just have to figure out how to get yourselves into the castle.

While considering options—Fleck has some intriguing ideas about grappling hooks and Boris is strongly in favor of any plan that includes hiding inside a wooden horse—you're interrupted by a visitor. A small army of visitors, rather—six large men on horseback, each with a hand twitching on the hilt of a mean-looking blade.

"You must be the demons that murdered Lord Fenwick and lay claim to his lands," one of them says, barely bothering to look at you.

"Murdered?" you say. "Um, actually, it was a chivalrous duel in accordance with—"

The horseman cuts you off. "We care not. Do you hereby swear fealty to the divine ruler, His Majesty King William Rufus the Definitely Sane?"

Boris jumps to his feet. "Swear fealty to a tyrant! I'd sooner—"

He lets out a small yelp as Fleck gives him a swift kick in the shin. "What the good knight means," you say, "is of course we do. Long live King Rufus!"

"Then you are expected at the royal residence tomorrow noon with tribute," he says. "Come alone, just the two of you, or bring the child to carry treasure if you must. Bring no additional guards."

He pauses as if contemplating his own craftiness. "It's not

(continue to the next page)

a trap," he adds at last before galloping off with his entourage.

"Do you think it's a trap?" Boris says as soon as they're gone.

"I think it might be," you agree.

"It's still our best chance," he insists. "We show up, depose the madman, fix the timeline, and disappear into the timestream before anyone's the wiser!"

Fleck isn't sold on the idea. "Or we sneak into the castle tonight under cover of darkness before they're expecting us," she says. She opens her eyes as wide as she can and whispers "*graaaaaaappling hooooooks.*"

"Sounds risky," Boris says. "I fear we'd be caught and killed before we can even *find* the king."

▶ *If you prefer the dog-faced time traveler's direct approach,* **turn to page 20.**

▶ *If you'd rather go full-on medieval ninja,* **turn to page 113.**

"Sorry, Captain," you say. "But I'm a lone wolf. A loose cannon. I roll *solo*."

You press the button on your time bracelet, but nothing happens. Whoops.

"I was afraid that might be the case," Captain Steele says. "Of course, our shielding prevents unauthorized time jumps. Let's get you to a guest room until we can decide whether or not it's safe to return you to the timestream."

The captain's "guest room" turns out to be an eight-foot by six-foot cell with a small cot that's nowhere near sturdy enough to support your tyrannoid physique. You sit on the floor without food or water for roughly twelve hours. It only takes you about four to start freaking completely the hell out.

Your cell door finally opens, and you're greeted by an unexpected visitor. It's Professor Velociraptor, dressed as always in casual businesswear and a lab coat, but looking twenty years older than you're used to seeing her. You're about 70 percent sure that she's a hallucination.

(continue to the next page)

"There you are!" she says. "Quick, we don't have much time!"

"You're TIME TRAVELERS." As long as you're talking to imaginary future professors, you may as well argue imaginary science. "Why would you ever have to RUSH TO DO ANYTHING?"

"Because, at any moment, you could shift into another dimension where I'm not dinofolk." She explains that Time Patrol Headquarters is built into a pocket dimension that moves sideways through reality instead of forward in time. She's been working here as their chief scientist for two decades, but she's the only one who isn't peeled off of space-time. So every time she greets any of her colleagues, they're shocked by her appearance since they've just shifted in from a reality where she evolved from something else entirely.

Yeah, you're *definitely* hallucinating. Professor V. kneels down and makes some adjustments to your bracelet.

"I'm sending you to the 1880s," she says. "The Time Patrol is working a case there, but in this instance, I don't think their interests and ours overlap. We're getting temporal signatures on a catastrophic scale, and I'm fairly certain that your mad scientist is involved somehow. The interdimensional time goblins *definitely* are."

Your confused expression must not fill her with confidence because she grabs you by the head and locks her gaze with yours.

"It's up to you to safeguard the dino-timeline," she says. "If you get into trouble, go back to my lab at the Time Travel Investigation Agency. Don't try to return here."

▶ Turn to page 8.

You push the button and send your ship hurtling through a massive time portal and into the dead quiet of empty space on the other side. Krikri rushes over and gives you a big hug. "Excellent work! Now we can clear the field and get you home."

In response to her enthusiasm, your armband emits a shower of sparks and a plume of thick, black smoke. You pull it off before it scorches your wrist, but the thing is completely shot. Creating such a large portal must have been too much for it.

To make matters worse, your commandeered goblin craft is in rough shape as well. You've got limited maneuverability and a few hours of life support at the absolute most. Plus, the craft was designed to dock inside a larger ship, so it has no landing gear whatsoever.

"If I can manage to get us to solid ground, it'll be a one-way trip," Krikri says. She fiddles with the console and frowns. "I do have communications, though. The custodians' base has gone silent, which can't be a good sign. We can attempt a landing, but I'm not sure what we'll find."

"What about Earth? Can we make it there before we run out of oxygen?"

"I think so," she says. "But whether the ship will survive a trip through the planet's atmosphere remains to be seen. We've got to put this thing down *somewhere*, though. Sooner than later."

▶ *If you attempt to land in the moonbase,*
    turn to page 180.

▶ *If you'd rather head for Earth,* **turn to page 120.**

Whether it's compassion, self-interest, or some mix of both, you choose life and prepare for the impending miracle of birth. Before too long you're the proud mother of eight rambunctious Labrador retriever puppies, and thanks to your fierce protection and tireless vigilance, every single one of them reaches adulthood.

It's a hard life but a good one. And eventually, a third generation sprouts up as well. (We realize this means some uncomfortable familial relations are going down, but they're dogs, you know? Grosser things have happened.) In fact, a large breed of domesticated canine proves surprisingly adaptable to the rigors of the late Cretaceous period. Your warm blood makes your species well-suited to the coming changes in climate, and the only other mammals to be found are small, rodent-like things that make an ideal food source for your progeny. In the centuries to come, your descendants spread out over the globe, being fruitful and multiplying anywhere the delicious little critters can be found.

See? Everything works out great! What possible catastrophic damage to the timeline could emerge from *that*?

The End

You leap toward your doppelganger—who, by the way, is *really* beginning to get on your nerves—and collide into Bruxelles, who has chosen this very moment to execute a flying roundhouse kick. It's nice to know that he went with non-lethal force, but even so, his foot smacks into your big dinosaur head and knocks you into your double just as the time machine screeches to life.

The room explodes in a technicolor light show. Wow, motorcycle-based time travel is significantly louder than armband-based time travel. You scramble to get your arms around your alternate self, who has a white-knuckle grip on the bike's handlebars.

Your double gives you a wild grin. "Sorry, but you must be THIS AWESOME to enjoy this ride."

You're treated a close-up view of an identical copy of your own foot and soon find yourself whirling helplessly through the vortex of time. Your guts feel like they're spinning in the opposite direction, and all you can do is curl up into a ball and try not to scream. After what might be a very short moment or pretty much forever, the vertigo subsides and you crack one eye open. You're crouched on the floor in Professor V.'s lab, and your boss is looking down at you, a time portal just closing behind her.

She gives you a little frown. "You didn't kill your alternate self in the past, did you?"

"No, I…" Wait a minute. What *did* happen? Your memory of the last few minutes is going all crazy. You remember Professor Velociraptor giving you some kind of time bracelet, but then, another version of you came—was it through a portal or on a motorcycle?—and tackled you. And then smashed the

(continue to the next page)

bracelet. Then some crazy monkey guy showed up and all you could think about was stealing his time machine, so you did, but your doppelganger jumped on board and... wait, was it you who fell off the bike, or the other one?

Either way, your stomach feels like it won't be able to handle solid food for a week, and you're considerably more ambivalent toward any alternate versions of yourself who may be bouncing around the space-time continuum.

"Okay, one more try," Professor V. says. "You're the only one who can do this. If you don't manage to peel yourself off the timestream, the very universe we inhabit could disappear forever."

▶ Turn to page 12.

War, it turns out, is hell. Who knew?

You give the order to your army to lay down arms, which isn't actually all that different from continuing to fight anyway, considering that the arms in question are mostly snapping like twigs when used against armored horsemen. Knights storm your encampment and take you prisoner as leader of the uprising. In the end, only half of your peasant soldiers survive the battle, but at least that's 5,000 more than would have lived if you had told them to keep fighting.

It gives you the tiniest sliver of comfort as you lay awake in your cell, waiting to be beheaded in the morning.

The End

Sure, why not? You like stuff that's unspeakably evil. You decide that your best hope of getting out of this mothership alive is by journeying into the heart of darkness, so you dive right in. And instantly realize that you've made a huge mistake. As you float weightlessly in the empty space between realities, thousands—nay, MILLIONS—of goblins crawl through rifts in space-time and surround you. You can sense the malevolence coming off them like stink.

The technology you've brought with you is useless here. Crap. The swarm draws nearer (you have no idea how they can even move because, without anything to push against, all you can do is float helplessly). Wait! Several of their creepy goblin holes open up within arm's reach. If you can spin yourself enough to get a limb into one of them, maybe you could grab something on the other side and pull yourself through?

You might as well give it a shot. I've got to warn you, though, this isn't going to turn out well. Go ahead and pick one at random, but you might as well keep your finger on this page because they range from disappointing to catastrophic. In fact, it would be easier for everyone if you just stayed here and let the goblins have you.

Seriously, none of those things lead anywhere you want to be.

▶ If you choose the first random, goblin-infested hole,
   turn to page 114.

▶ If the second one looks like the hole for you,
   turn to page 156.

▶ If you like the cut of the third hole's jib,
   turn to page 250.

You tell Cornelia that you'd prefer to get to know each other better before sharing the secrets of space and time. She seems irritated but is apparently willing to play along. So you spin a dramatic tale of the future that cobbles together the basic plots of *Star Wars*, *The Matrix*, and *Stargate: Atlantis*.

Beatrice, in particular, is transfixed by your story and eager to talk. From her, you learn that the sisters A) employ several time traveling scientists, B) have a giant, prehistoric ancestor of modern Tyrannosaurus rex in their basement, which they use for God knows what, and C) keep their most sensitive equipment not in the compound itself, but in a huge airship that floats above the city. All told, her story might be even more unbelievable than yours.

"That's why we're not worried about the Gas Can Gang," she says. "Any day now, the ship should be ready for—ow!"

Her sister kicks her in the shin, hard. "I believe that's enough for now, Beatrice. Surely our guest grows tired of all this chatter."

You're a bit surprised that you learned as much as you did and figure you'd best not push your luck. "Indeed," you say. "Perhaps we can continue this conversation another day?" It's worth a shot. There's no way they'll let you just walk out of here, though, is there?

"Certainly," Cornelia says. "Horse, show our new friend to the door."

You can hardly believe your luck. Now that you've confirmed that you have a time machine, she must have decided that a more-flies-with-honey approach is her best play. You have no idea why, since you've already proven how well you respond

(continue to the next page)

to threats of violence.

"Oh, but you can't leave already!" Beatrice says. "At least come and meet the Reverse Engineer. His era doesn't have blue pills or Wraith Queens or such wonders, but you *must* hear his tales of the Cube of Rubix and the Flocks of Seagulls. I know you'll get along fabulously."

Wait. *Rubik's Cube?* That sounds like the 1980s to you. Could this Reverse Engineer person be the mad scientist you're searching for? If so, maybe you should stick around and look into it. On the other hand, you notice that Cornelia is giving her sister the stink-eye something fierce. Perhaps you'd better go report back while you still have the chance.

▶ *If you get out while the getting's good,*
   turn to page 86.

▶ *If you tell Beatrice you'd love to meet her engineer,*
   turn to page 178.

Dolphins? *Really?* The whole central joke of this book is that because the universe changed around you before you were peeled off of space-time, you don't remember that you used to be a human and think people had always evolved from dinosaurs. So now, when forced to pick which timeline survives, you go with a third, unrelated timeline? I mean, every decision you make here is valid. There are no right or wrong answers. But I have to tell you this particular choice turns out…

Awesome! Seriously, YOU ARE THE BEST AT CHOOSE YOUR OWN ADVENTURES. Krikri, it turns out, is from the future. Like, way, *way* in the future, after human beings manage to bungle themselves to extinction and dolphins become the dominant lifeform. The thing is, regardless of which species evolves to take over the planet in your era—dinosaurs, primates, Labrador retrievers, houseplants, whatever—they all meet their end pretty much the same way, setting the stage for the eventual dolphin utopia. So reflected in Krikri's soulful little dolphin eyes *isn't just one timeline*. It's every timeline where any living thing evolves to the point of sentience at all.

And by telling the Persistent Universe to save her, you just managed to save all of it.

You win!

THE END

"I'll go too," Krikri says. "You'll need my help to dial in the machine."

Your mind clouds a bit as half of it slips away, and soon you're back to your singular, mammalian consciousness. You feel your host's rage building. Agh! You forgot how difficult it was to control this thing. You also forgot *how hungry you are.*

"I'll return as soon as we know anything," Krikri says. She disappears with a soft pop, and your group is reduced to Bruxelles, yourself, and a single Hercule Von Krumpf, looking roughly 300 times more sane than each of the ranting madmen who recently beamed directly into his brain.

As far as you're concerned, Krikri can take as long as she wants. The monster inside you has been kept quiet long enough. You embrace the hunger, and focus on the twisted army of goblins outside that will finally sate your ravenous—

"I'm back!"

Wow, that was fast. But of course it would be. Krikri could take weeks on her trip to the future and still return the moment she left—that's how time travel works. You realize that the same goes for your other half, yet you don't feel your alternate-universe memories returning. One sorrowful glance from Krikri tells you everything you need to know.

The other you didn't make it.

Krikri gets down to brass tacks. "The goblins live in the spaces between timelines," she says, "and can't create alternate timelines by making decisions the way we do. What I mean is that normally whenever any sentient being makes a choice, the universe splits into two. It happens millions of times per second, causing an ever-growing, infinite number of realities."

(continue to the next page)

Okay, that sounds… insane.

"But the goblins can't split the universe," she continues. "They don't belong to any reality at all. When they try to make a decision, they just split *themselves*, then go ahead and do both."

You've been there. "But what does that have to do with us?"

"Well, they were once normal people in a normal universe until a tachyon event of astronomical proportions collapsed their reality."

"The tower!" Hercule says. "At full power, the tachyon discharge would be immense. I designed it to vent into an alternate reality, so it wouldn't…" he trails off. "My God, is all of this *my* fault?"

"They're sending a comet to stop you from doing it!" you say.

Krikri shakes her head. "They're sending a comet to *ensure* he does it. The goblins caused the dinosaur extinction, which caused Hercule to build his machine to stop it, which in turn brought them into existence in the first place, so they could cause the dinosaur extinction." It's one of those self-inducing chronology loops you've always dreaded encountering. If your boss makes you write up the paperwork on this one, you're going to be *pissed*.

Hercule opens a tattered notebook and starts frantically scribbling equations in it with a stubby pencil. "I can reroute the tachyons," he says. "If I saturate the beam with them, it won't have to vent anywhere and should create enough energy to vaporize the comet. Two birds with one stone! The dinosaurs never go extinct, and the goblin timeline never collapses!"

"I don't think it works that way," Krikri says. "They exist

(continue to the next page)

outside causality now. Nothing we do will stop them. And they'll keep coming—their numbers are potentially infinite. This is a suicide mission."

"I've got to try," he says. You're impressed with his determination. His filthy beard and tattered clothing still make him look like a street person, but fused-together, sane Von Krumpf seems willing to risk his life to set things right. "I still have my time machine. I'll open up a portal for anyone who doesn't want to be a part of this."

You realize that you probably should have had a couple of clones remove their own machines before disintegrating so you had a spare or two. You've got more pressing concerns at the moment, however. The half of you from the dino-timeline is gone. In your universe, people evolved from mammals. If Hercule does manage to blow up the comet, and the dinosaurs never go extinct, what happens to *you*? Will you still exist with new memories of a world filled with dinosaur people?

Or will you just... *disappear*?

▶ *If you tell Von Krumpf you'd like to get out while the getting's good,* **turn to page 124.**

▶ *If you stay and take your chances with the suicide mission (double suicide? If the universe doesn't delete you, the goblins surely will),* **turn to page 91.**

"I give up! Please stop hitting me!" It's not the most dignified surrender, but the important thing is that the punishment ends. You cautiously unclench your eyes and see your assailant hunched over, its big metal head just inches from your face.

"Future technology detected," it says, clamping a little clockwork gizmo onto your wristband before you can pull your arm away. "Dampener engaged."

Uh oh. Before you have the chance to examine your time bracelet, the automaton heaves you to your feet and prods you with its billy club until you start walking. Any attempt to fiddle with the armband results in a sharp rap on the wrist, which quickly trains you to keep your hands at your sides. After a short march, you find yourself at the entrance to an imposing stone building. Before you know it, you're being lifted by the scruff of your neck, carried down a rough-hewn staircase and thrown head-first into a dark, unfurnished chamber with iron bars on the door. You smack your head on the stone floor and pass out.

When you eventually wake up, a thin shaft of sunlight wafts in from a tiny, barred window high up on one wall of your cell. You're sore *everywhere*. You examine your time bracelet but find that it's been rendered inert. Every time you press a button or even touch the little doohickey that your mechanical jailor attached to it, you're jolted with a nasty electric shock. You try banging it against the wall of your cell, but the dampener is at least as sturdy as the bracelet itself and apparently stuck on there with glue or something. Any attempt to destroy it seems just as likely to break the whole thing.

"Nice piece of future tech you've got there, friend."

(continue to the next page)

You see a small, porthole-sized window in one wall of the chamber. A smallish, pink arm is waving at you through the bars in it, accompanied by a woman's voice. "Here, let me see. I might be able to use it to get us out of here!"

You're not sure if this is a fellow prisoner or some elaborate ruse to fool you into giving up your secrets. But either way, handing over your only hope of ever escaping of this century seems like a bad idea.

"You're out of luck," you say, "because I can't even take it off my wrist without getting electrocuted."

"That's the tech dampener," the mystery woman says. "I can bypass that. Shove your whole arm through the bars! Quickly— someone's coming!" Sure enough, you hear a door open and close, followed by a clanking that sounds like the policebot clambering down the stairs.

"They'll kill you to get their hands on that thing," the voice says. "This is our only chance—you have to trust me!"

Do you, though?

▶ *If you trust the pink-armed lady in the next cell and stick your arm through the bars,* **turn to page 251.**

▶ *If you take your chances with the policebot,* **turn to page 62.**

You go with Velox, who transports you to an enormous amphitheater with majestic views of a dark, sunless moonscape. An eclectic army of time travelers is assembling.

Although this base belongs to Velox's Temporal Custodians, the interdimensional time goblins' forces have decimated their numbers, and fewer than twenty remain. The largest faction represented in the hall is the Time Patrol—the two groups are chrono-enforcement organizations from entirely different

(continue to the next page)

eras and are easy to distinguish since the former are uniformly dressed in silver jumpsuits with shaved heads while the latter sport leather jackets and terrible '80s hair. With the way their members eyeball each other, you gather that there's no love lost between them.

Other assembled forces include an exuberant gentleman with the head of a Labrador retriever, some kind of winged centaur thing, and twelve or thirteen middle-aged white guys with questionable fashion sense. One of them is wearing a *fez*.

"You'll be assigned to Jurassic Squadron," Velox says, introducing you to an assembly of humanoid T. rexes who… *appear to be identical to you in every way.*

Well, not entirely identical. Through a bit of uncomfortable small talk, you discover that your recent experiences differ considerably. One of you survived the goblin invasion here on the moon while another came directly from the Middle Ages. One explored the 1880s, and another was held captive by the Time Patrol after refusing to join their ranks. You're even joined by a naked, 20-foot-tall, prehistoric T. rex, which you're not sure entirely fits in with the group.

That is, until it speaks (in a voice that, though deeper and more gravelly, you immediately recognize as your own). "Seriously, *eleven bucks an hour*. I am *not* properly trained for this."

A somewhat older version of you wears the leather jacket of the Time Patrol and an honest-to-God eye patch. "I've been in some tough scrapes in my days, but *this*… I've got to admit, I've never seen anything like it."

That isn't reassuring. You turn your attention to the stage

(continue to the next page)

where the leaders of your ragtag army have gathered: Velox, Captain Francesca Steele of the Time Patrol, Krikri the Dolphin Lady, and Professor Vegetatious, who seems to communicate only by shaking leafy appendages. Which, of course, none of you can understand.

Captain Steele addresses the crowd. "Ladies. Gentlemen." She nods at the professor. "Plant monsters. We've battled the time goblin horde through all of history. But here, on the surface of the moon, our enemies have chosen to make their final assault on the fabric of reality itself. And it's here that we make our stand."

Gulp.

"Our plan is simple," Captain Steele continues. "An all out assault on the goblin stronghold around the gateway to the Great Consciousness of the Persistent Universe."

"Which we never should have abandoned in the first place," Velox mutters.

"Which we were *forced* to retreat from, much to our dismay," Krikri says. "The problem is, the goblins have erected an energy shield around the gate, which our technology cannot penetrate."

Captain Steele clears her throat. "We have no choice but to send a contingent to the goblin mothership to take out the shield's power source," she says. "We'll need the bulk of our numbers for the main assault, so we can only spare a few of you. Your chances of success won't be great. And I have to be honest with you: chances of *survival* are even worse."

Grizzled Time Patrol Veteran You raises a tiny arm. "Jurassic Squadron volunteers."

(continue to the next page)

Wait. *What?*

"If this is indeed the will of the council, then the Legion of Time Traveling tyrannosaurs will see it done. You have my raygun."

"And my axe."

"And my, uh… cell phone, I guess."

One by one, your other selves offer various weapons and utensils to the cause. Then they all turn to you expectantly. Wow. That's some *serious* peer pressure. You can't be the only dinosaur who doesn't volunteer for the suicide mission, can you?

▶ *Sure you can! If you silently edge your way toward some other squadron,* **turn to page 122.**

▶ *If you suck it up and stick with the group,* **turn to page 60.**

"Everyone, calm down," you say. "I'm not a dragon! I'm just a... *traveler*. From really, *really* far away."

"It talks! Kill the talking dragon!"

Sigh. "Listen, I'm not here to hurt anyone." You take a step backward, away from the crowd and toward an empty, muddy expanse. "I'm just going to back away slowly, okay? Nobody make any sudden moves."

"Kill it! Quick, before it steals our mud!"

"I'm not going to steal your *mud*. I promise."

A small child pokes her head—*his* head? Gender is impossible to determine under the layers of burlap and grime—out from behind her mother's apron. "Please, your dragonousness," the child says. "*The mud is all we have.*"

As you ponder this, you hear the clip-clop of hooves and metal clanking on metal. A mounted knight appears from behind one of the half-collapsed structures, decked out in plate mail armor that's been polished to a gleam.

"Save us, Lord Protector!" someone yells from the rabble.

"Well, you're certainly an ugly one," the knight chuckles, pulling off his helmet to get a better look at you. "You didn't come from that godforsaken cave, did you?" He has a meticulously-trimmed blonde bowl cut, a pointed nose and a strong chin. There's a certain tone in the knight's laughter that does not inspire your trust. You note that the ornate etchings on his armor match the barding on his horse, which mirrors its master's haughty stare.

To be honest, even his horse looks like an asshole.

"Reports from the countryside seem to have been... *exaggerated*," the knight says. "You're not *nearly* as large as they say.

(continue to the next page)

Well, no matter. You're here gathering meat to get you through the winter, I suppose? Fair enough. How many of these wretched peasants do you require to leave our lands unmolested?"

What? Classy guy, this Lord Protector. "I don't want the peasants," you say.

"So you *are* here for the mud." The knight's glare hardens, and he draws an enormous, sharp-looking sword from a horse-mounted scabbard. "I'm afraid I can't let you have it."

"The *mud* is more valuable than the *people*?"

"Of course," he says. "There are already more of them than needed to work the mud fields, and they breed like vermin." He rears back on his horse and points his weapon at you. The townsfolk scatter. "Now, if you have any begging for mercy to do, I suggest you do it quickly before I cleave you in two."

That would seem to take begging for mercy off the table as far as options go. Aren't knights supposed to obey some kind of chivalrous code? Maybe if you can convince him that you're a knight as well, he'll at least give you a sword to defend yourself with. Then again, you look at the giant blade he's wielding in one hand and wonder if you could even lift it.

He seems to genuinely believe you're some kind of mythological creature, though. Can you capitalize on that? From what you know of history, medieval denizens were quite the superstitious lot.

▶ *If you challenge him to a proper duel according to the code of chivalry,* **turn to page 69.**

▶ *If you play up the dragon angle and bluff him with firebreathing and whatnot,* **turn to page 264.**

You really do want to safeguard the multiverse from an insane inventor who could be out who knows where, who knows when, doing irreparable damage to the timestream. But nevertheless, killing alternate versions of yourself just feels wrong. Maybe it's the sleeping, defenseless thing that's bugging you. You think back to the doppelganger in Professor V.'s lab—who, frankly, was starting to annoy the crap out of you—and decide it would definitely be easier to kill that one.

Before you can bring up the possibility to Bruxelles, however, a second motorcycle screeches into the room with a second Bruxelles and a third you in tow. The sleeping doppelganger awakes with a start, screams, and runs out of the room. The other double (triplet?) hops off the bike and points a gun at your head.

You grab the attacking T. rex by the arm in a blind panic. Both Chances sigh. "It has to be this way," one of them says. "You wanted to do it with a waking double instead of the sleeping one, so here we are. Just relax, my friend. It is the only way."

Is it, though? IS IT? One thing's for sure: being on this side of the time-shifted-alternate-self-killing *sucks*. But you're certainly having a hard time pulling the trigger yourself. Maybe you should just let a future version do the heavy lifting, murder-wise?

▶ *Oh, hell no! If you fight tooth and nail until your dying breath,* **turn to page 131.**

▶ *You know what? Fine. Someone has to be the murderee, so if you decide it might as well be you,* **turn to page 270.**

There's something about those glowing blue portals you just can't resist. So long, Middle Ages! You make the jump again and find yourself on a gaslit city street. From the cobblestone pavement and smokestacks belching black smoke into the atmosphere, you'd guess you've landed somewhere in the late 1800s.

You have to admit that you're disappointed. After prehistoric jungles and the medieval countryside, you're having trouble imagining what kind of life you might carve out for yourself during the friggin' Cleveland administration. As you ponder your options, a pair of odd contraptions marches up the street. They're roughly eight feet tall and built of iron with exposed gears and jets of steam venting from the tops of their heads.

Hold on. Is this the *steampunk* 1800s? With clockwork automatons, airship pirates, and the whole nine yards? That's a different story entirely! This is *awesome*!

"Warning! Citizenry restricted to housing after curfew!" one of them says in mechanical tones. Before you have a chance to protest (or, you know, *roar*, since protesting isn't actually in your repertoire these days), you're hit with an electric shock that pulses through your entire dinosaur nervous system and leaves you momentarily unable to move.

"Warning!" the thing continues. "Surrender or suffer the full force of law!"

Surrender? You're T. rex, monarch of the Cretaceous! Terror of medieval Europe! You're not about to surrender to—

With the second shock, all seven tons of you slumps to the ground.

▶ *If you surrender,* **turn to page 28.**

▶ *If you rage against the clockwork machine,*
   turn to page 158.

That guy clearly doesn't want to give you a ride. And anyway, didn't he say something about exploding? You decide to stick it out here in 2271 with Krikri. She'll help you! After all, she's never let you down before.

As you approach your friend, you start to realize that something is wrong. For starters, even though you call out to her, she remains completely still. Also, the closer you get, the more you realize that she's bigger than she should be. Krikri wasn't… *twelve feet tall*, was she?

Son of a bitch. It's a freaking *statue* of Krikri. Apparently, at some point in the future they start painting marble statues in lifelike colors. The plaque beneath it reads, *"Dedicated to Krikri the Dolphin Lady, friend to all time travelers, for unequaled bravery and distinction in the field of chrono-enforcement."*

Alas, whatever she did to earn that distinction doesn't include ever returning to 2271 to rescue your sorry ass.

You die alone.

THE END

You look at Annie as if she just took something you didn't even know was in your heart and made it real. "You had me at *ornithoptivelocipede*," you say.

She starts preparing her contraptions for launch, and you help her charge them with your bracelet. The process consists of hooking tubes up to both machines to transfer an invisible, odorless gas that may or may not entirely exist in your plane of reality. But it makes the little dials on the engines go from "empty" to "full," and that's good enough for you.

It's a treat to see Annie in her element, adjusting machinery at breakneck pace and wielding an enormous, three-foot wrench with the precision of a surgeon. "I can see why they call you *Gearbox*," you say.

"What? Oh, that's not how I got my nickname." She raps on the lacing of her corset with her knuckles, which makes an unexpected tinny, hollow sound.

Your mouth drops open. "But... you're..."

"An automaton?" She laughs. "Naw. At least, not save for a few select parts. My parents, God rest their souls, were fabulously well-to-do but also profoundly vain. You can imagine, then, their consternation when their youngest daughter came out... *faulty.*"

If Annie is troubled by these memories, it doesn't show. "I spent my childhood confined to the attic rooms of our estate. Partially for my own well-being, of course—in my youth I was far from the hearty specimen you see before you—but also, I think, so my family wouldn't have to acknowledge me in polite society. Fortunately, the attic was also where they kept my grandfather's library, which included the most extensive

(continue to the next page)

collection of scientific knowledge in the western hemisphere."

She taps her left leg, which, under her petticoats, makes a satisfying metallic thump. "I devoured the tomes and was conducting my own experiments by the age of six. As far as my physical handicaps, I managed to straighten myself out in good time," she says. "Remind me to show you the mess of gearworks I've got running up and down my spine. Anyway, by the time my own intestines betrayed me, I had a replacement set all worked up. Eve of my seventeenth birthday, if I correctly recall." Wow. You had assumed that all of the weirdly advanced technology you've seen here was brought in by time travelers but, apparently, at least some of it is home-grown.

It's nearly midnight by the time Annie finishes fiddling with her engines and snaps her goggles from the brim of her hat down over her eyes.

"Let's ride."

There are only three ornithoptivelocipedes, so the six of you double up. Cartwright refuses to even consider going unless she can ride with Annie, which leaves you and Bobbins each with a Powder Monkey. The things aren't designed with seatbelts, but lashing yourself to the frame with a length of rope gets the job done. Safety first! It's long after curfew, and the abandoned street outside makes a functional runway. You roll out, steady your handlebars, flip the lever to engage the motor, and gently push on the foot pedal. The machine's wings flap wildly, and rather than moving forward as you expected, you lurch into the sky at a 45 degree angle. Woohoo! You're flying!

It's everything you could ever dream of and more. After a few minutes getting comfortable with the controls—which

(continue to the next page)

mostly consist of "flap more" and "flap less" with the slightest bit of steering thrown in—you follow the others into the dense black cloud cover. You hold your breath as you pass through to avoid a lungful of soot (environmental regulations in this era are appalling) and get visual confirmation of your target in the moonlight the moment you emerge from the darkness. You have no idea how big the average dirigible is supposed to be, but this one is absolutely colossal.

As you approach, two small, fixed-wing aircraft drop from beneath the passenger compartment and glide toward you. They're unmanned and similar in design to the clockwork policebot you had trouble with yesterday, fitted for flight rather than crowd control. Annie and Bobbins veer off to either side, and the bogeys change course to intercept them.

"Stay on target!" Annie yells just before she's out of earshot. You do, and fortunately, no third defender materializes. Soon, you're spitting distance from the airship and see that the hatch the robot planes launched from remains open.

"DISRUPTOR OR CONCUSSION?" your Powder Monkey passenger yells in your ear above the howling wind.

"WHAT?" you yell back.

"WHICH BOMB," he hollers (you have Skip, incidentally, the little boy Monkey). "SHORT CIRCUIT OR BIG BOOM?"

You realize that you should have planned all of this before launch. Perhaps the disruptor bomb will short out any automatic defenses, allowing you to board the ship? Then again, the whole point is to take it down. Should you just go all in?

▶ *If you tell your Powder Monkey to toss the disruptor bomb,* **turn to page 186.**

▶ *If it's concussive all the way,* **turn to page 278.**

You understand that we're trying to give you the chance to back out, right? So you don't wind up getting yourself killed on, like, your second choice in this thing?

- ▶ *Fine, I'll go back into the stupid dog.* **Turn to page 16.**

- ▶ *Wait, I mean the dinosaur! The dinosaur is clearly the better idea!* **Turn to page 34.**

- ▶ *Did I stutter? I said I'm finding a different host body. And you can't tell me what to do.* **Turn to page 13.**

The voice in your head said something about being forced into a decision that would peel the universe off of itself? It wasn't super clear. But if you're going to cancel that particular apocalypse, you decide you'd better make your stand here.

"We stay and fight!"

Velox looks at you with pride and steadfast determination. Then a beam of light envelops her, and she's gone.

Uh oh.

Soon the entire chamber is a sea of red as hundreds of beams burst through the ceiling at once. One catches you, and frankly, we've got some good news and bad news for you here.

The good news is that it's not a death ray! Those things have been transport beams all along! The bad news is that the inter-dimensional time goblins have stopped screwing around and transport you directly into the vacuum of space. Your desperate attempt to activate the time machine on your wrist yields no results—whatever Velox did to disable it is still in effect.

Contrary to popular wisdom, you don't explode, or freeze solid, or boil, or anything weird like that. But you do lose consciousness in about fourteen seconds and suffocate soon afterward.

THE END

You wriggle out of your captors' arms, hurl yourself into the portal, and crash right into the mad scientist in mid-timewarp. He lets out a demented wail and starts buffeting you wildly with his arms. Although your diminutive T. rex hands aren't particularly useful for zero-G slapfighting, you manage to get a grip on the time bracelet with your teeth and wrest it away from him. Then, you use your tail to shove off and distance yourself from your flailing adversary.

The scientist screams and disappears, re-entering the timestream at some unknown point in history. Crud. Well, at least wherever he winds up, he won't have your time machine. You continue through the vortex for a moment, then lurch back into normal space-time with a jolt.

Rather than the expected shimmering portal, you're floating in a featureless white room. A bald, shapely primate-woman in a silver jumpsuit glares at you disapprovingly. "Your presence in this timeline is unauthorized," she says. "No one travels to or from the 2270s without explicit permission from the Temporal Custodians of the Persistent Universe."

You push the button on your time travel bracelet, but no shimmering portal appears. Damnit! What is the *deal* with that thing? You're not sure what's going on here, so you keep quiet and wait for her to continue.

"We serve the living force that flows through every corner of reality, throughout all eternity," she says. "It's nothing less than the self-aware, omniscient expression of existence itself."

Um, okay. "I don't think that sounds like a real thing," you say.

▶ Turn to page 64.

Gas Can Rebellion or no, you've still got an entire time-line full of dinofolk to save, and you're not going to accomplish that by getting yourself blown up. You veer left, scoot past the switch and try to find some cover, since bullets are still flying and avoiding them is priority number one. Priority number two is getting the hell off this godforsaken dirigible.

The fates are with you (at first, anyway). You make your way back to the chamber where you left your flying machine and, with a pang of guilt for leaving your companions behind, jump on it and push yourself out the hatch. It turns out that piloting an ornithoptivelocipede starting from a dead freefall is extra tricky, but you manage to pull out of your nosedive and straighten up just before hitting the city streets below.

As far as daring escapes go, it's as impressive as hell. Alas, it's all for naught. Remember that glowing orb in the airship hundreds of feet above you? It goes off. And you never find out what its intended purpose is because its blast radius is some-thing like 3,000 miles, which is enough to decimate pretty much all of the United States, Canada, and Mexico.

You get yourself blown up after all.

THE END

You have no idea what's going on in this weird, funhouse-mirror version of 1882, but you decide that the situation calls for caution. You observe from the alleyway, where you figure you'll be safe, at least until you've gathered some more information.

At this point, two things happen at once. First, one of the kids pulls some kind of gadget out of a burlap sack and tosses it at the robot policeman, where it adheres to the thing's metallic hide and promptly explodes. It collapses into a pile of junk while the children skitter away around a corner.

Second, a futuristic motorcycle appears out of nowhere, crashes right into you, and kills you instantly.

Here's the thing about surfing the timestream: THERE IS NO PLAYING IT SAFE. Anything could happen! Out of nowhere! I'm not saying that was the universe punishing you for standing by and watching while two small children get beaten up by a robot or anything (after all, they took care of themselves fine). But, you know. Sometimes things happen for a reason.

That's a little time travel lesson for you there.

THE END

In one last, desperate plea for lucidity, you hurl your consciousness back into the past, and this time, when you see the goblin emerge from its interdimensional crevice, you float as fast as you can in the opposite direction. It's quicker than you are, though, and by the time you reach the tower, Chance is already fully engaged with the goblin masses. You catch a glimpse of Krikri just as she disappears into the future.

You throw yourself into the T. rex's head but find no comfort there. The madness eclipses your other self's sanity as readily as it did yours, and soon, your companions can add an utterly cracked and *extremely* hungry tyrannosaur to their troubles.

Needless to say, it doesn't end well.

THE END

Maybe it's those inexplicably sincere dolphin eyes, or the fact that she was vouched for by a really enthusiastic disembodied voice, but you decide to follow Krikri and hope for the best. If it turns out to be a disintegrator beam, though, and atomizes you on the spot, you're going to be *pissed*.

You jump into the column of light and immediately find yourself in a cramped, dimly lit chamber. Transporter beam! *Yes!* Then a small, gnarled creature leaps from out of the shadows and attacks you in the face. Aaaagh! You try to pull it off, but for its size, the thing is crazy strong. A second critter attaches itself to your torso, grabbing at your armband.

There's a crackle of electricity that blinds you for just a second, and suddenly both creatures are gone. As your vision returns, you see Krikri, armed with what looks like a glowing egg duct-taped to the end of a broom handle, zapping two more of the little buggers into oblivion.

(continue to the next page)

Well, that was one of the most terrifying things that you've ever experienced. "What *were* those things?" you ask.

Krikri is poking around the corners of the room, checking for stragglers. "Interdimensional time goblins," she says. "Or that's how I've heard them described, anyway, and it's as fitting a description as any. This is one of their ships."

She explains that the ships exist in multiple realities at once and cloak themselves psychically by convincing the human mind that such a thing is utterly impossible. The more willfully closed-minded the observer, the better the technology works.

You're absolutely bursting with questions, but before you can get to them, something hits the ship, rocking it momentarily back and forth. Krikri rushes to a display panel on the wall. "It's a tractor beam," she says. "The goblin mothership is pulling all the smaller ships in!"

You check your armband and find it still inoperable. "Can you get us out of here? My time machine seems to be on the fritz."

"That's the custodians' dampener field. My technology isn't affected, but I'm afraid I'm not equipped to carry passengers. We'll have to get past the edge of moonspace before you'll have access to the timestream. But if we make a run for it, the goblins will know something's wrong and try to shoot us down."

She gives you one of her soulful looks. "Our only other option is to let them take us, though. Which comes with its own set of problems."

▶ *If you let the mothership pull you in,* **turn to page 100.**

▶ *If you try to make it to the edge of the dampener field before they blast you out of the sky,* **turn to page 76.**

He's fully armored and seems pretty good with that spiked chain-ball thing, so you imagine he can work this out on his own. "Yeah, kill that demon!" you mutter, trying to blend in with the crowd as you edge away from the commotion.

Said commotion, however, is escalating rapidly. A small mob of townsfolk rushes past you brandishing some kind of hoe and pickaxe combination, one of which catches your disguise and pulls it right off of your back.

"Another demon!" someone yells in panic. "It's an invasion! Kill them! Kill them all!"

Somebody rips the cloak off of an old woman with a goiter, proclaims her to be a third demon, and runs away screaming. You try to appease the crowd and remind them that yesterday they decided you were a knight, but by that time, they're already whipped into a frenzy. You're hit in the back of the head with something sharp and heavy—pickaxe/hoe, perhaps?—and collapse into a heap in the mud. As the life seeps out of you, you wonder if the Labrador knight fared better than you did.

Alas, you never find out.

THE END

Chance will be fine. The only thing you've contributed to the partnership so far has been LITERALLY slowing him down. Plus, you've got your own mission, safeguarding the one *true* timeline, where people evolved from *dinosaurs*.

You hop out of the balloon's basket and drop safely to the ground (it's really not that far). You recover the time bracelet—which looks just like the one you surrendered back at Time Patrol HQ—and open yourself up a portal. You're aiming for the lab back in your own time period but aren't a hundred percent sure you've dialed it in correctly. Well, if you wind up in the wrong century, you can always try again, right?

The moment you're in the time tunnel, you realize something's wrong. Those freaky goblin creatures are in there with you! One of them attacks, trying to wrest your time bracelet from your arm. Hey! You *need* that! You manage to free yourself from the thing's clammy grasp just as you re-enter normal space-time.

You find yourself in the middle of a muddy village, surrounded by what look like medieval peasants. They're mammal-folk, like Chance and the people in the 1880s. "Dragon!" one of them yells. "Or monster, or something!"

Okay, this definitely isn't Professor V.'s lab. You hate to risk another time jump when those creatures are running loose in between portals, but it beats being lynched. You press a button on your bracelet...

And nothing happens. Damnit.

"Kill the dragon!" someone else screams.

▶ *If you calmly explain to the peasants that you're not a dragon monster, you're a human being,* **turn to page 226.**

▶ *If you skip the pleasantries and run,* **turn to page 80.**

You allow the growing crowd of lunatics to herd you into what is more or less their *lair*, even though there's no way this could possibly end well. The ground floor is one enormous metal chamber with a hodgepodge of consoles and switches lining the walls and a circular pit in the center. Yet another scientist awaits you there, this one with a beard at least a foot longer than the others. He looks like he hasn't slept in a year.

He sees you and does a double take. "The dog! Is it time for tests already?" He checks the digital clock on his time travel chest rig and gasps.

You scan the room for possible exits, but there's only the door you entered through, and it's packed with science clones. Meanwhile, the longbearded one has begun muttering to himself. "Mistakes were made," he says. "One trip to the Precambrian and suddenly the dinosaurs all lost their feathers! So much work to do—we doubled and redoubled once I understood I could travel back mere seconds, then immediately decide not to. The universe can't self-correct me! Persistent or otherwise, it holds no power if you can't hear its cry through the static."

You decide that Longbeard takes the medal for battiest clone so far (and that field was *competitive*). But before he can launch into a chorus of "I'm a Little Teapot," or wherever this is headed, a column of blue light erupts from the pit in the center of the room.

Apparently the crazy bastards have a death ray.

Someone grabs you from behind, and you yelp in surprise. "Don't worry, girl," Longbeard says. "The test can't hurt you. It only has the power to make you *whole*."

(continue to the next page)

Okay, that sounds like nonsense. "It seeks out the best possible version," he continues. "The one true *you*, anywhere in history, in any possible timeline. Two become one. Merged with your ideal self, you'll lead the life you were always meant to. This machine will send you where you *belong*."

His voice grows soft. "After all these years, it will finally bring you *home*."

You're pretty sure he's talking to the voices in his head at this point. Nevertheless, is there any chance this could be your ticket back to the twenty-first century? You're not sure if your job at the TTIA qualifies as the ideal you in any possible time-line, but if this contraption actually does anything like what he claims it will, it might be your only way home.

Before you get the opportunity to find out, though, a portal opens up across the room and another scientist steps through. "Nope," he says flatly. "The dog just exploded."

"I can fix that!" one of them yells from a console. "Okay, try it now!"

Your captor lifts you off the floor and carries you toward the beam. Nooooo! Wait, but if you were going to explode again, another clone would show up and make them recalibrate, right? So that means this time the device should work as advertised?

Either that or you blow up even worse, and they just give it up as a lost cause.

▶ *If you go gentle into that blue light,* **turn to page 103.**

▶ *If you freak out, bite your captor, and try to wriggle out of his grasp,* **turn to page 190.**

Wooooooo! Guns blazing! Always a solid plan. Annie and Bobbins spend most of the day siphoning what they insist is an invisible gas from your time bracelet into devices of various description. Meanwhile, Cartwright gives you a rundown of the attack plan.

"There are entrances here and here," she says, spreading a heavy canvas map of the compound out over a low wooden table. "We'll hit the main one since it's the most heavily guarded."

You can't argue with her logic there.

"With the firepower we're packing," she continues, "our best bet is to come at them fast and hard before they know what hit 'em. So we chuck a few aether bombs right here, then storm the compound and clean up the rest with repeating disruptor rifles and shock rods."

You can hardly wait to find out what repeating disruptor rifles and shock rods are. "I know it sounds grisly," Cartwright says, "but these men are hired thugs, and a particularly nasty bunch at that." She absentmindedly rubs a scar that runs the length of her left forearm. "They won't hesitate to put a bullet in you, so don't give 'em the opportunity."

"Our only hope is to secure the place quickly," Annie says, joining you at the table. "We need to capture or otherwise incapacitate the sisters and take control of their clockwork centurions before they can be called back to defend the compound. The automatons will be out on rounds at sunset, enforcing curfew, so we strike then."

It's a good plan and, as it turns out, well executed. The Powder Monkeys truly are wizards at detonation, and their aether bombs make short work of the compound's fortifications,

(continue to the next page)

not to mention the bulk of the guards. The remaining forces are outfitted with various clockwork weapons—some of which have apparently been grafted to their bodies—but Cartwright leads the way with a long staff that emits an electrical discharge, rendering their devices useless. The others work cleanup duty like a well-oiled machine. You don't even need to *use* your repeating disruptor rifle.

After a few minutes of carnage, you find what must be the control center. It's a huge, round room with various types of machinery lining the walls. Two statuesque women decked out in bustles and fancy hats are frantically twisting knobs and flipping switches.

"It's over," Annie says. "Step away from the control panel, both of you, and this doesn't have to end in bloodshed."

"Oh, Annabelle," one of them says. "Of course it does." She pulls a big lever that launches the pair of them straight up through a circular hatch in the ceiling, their ruffled petticoats aflutter. At the same instant, the door behind you slams shut, and a trapdoor in the center of the room opens with a clang.

Out of the trapdoor emerges an enormous metal creature shaped like a prehistoric T. rex. It's not clockwork, like the contraptions you've seen so far, but built from gleaming steel, like something out of a Japanese cartoon. Your weapons are useless against it.

You get eaten by a huge, robotic version of yourself.

THE END

Krikri is gracious about your decision and even offers to upload her own database of time travel research into the custodians' computers. She leaves, and you settle in for... well, let's call it an *extended* stay.

The bad news is, you're totally going to die on the moon. The good news is, you've still got sixty good years before you do. Over the coming decades, you give yourself an education in advanced mathematics and time travel theory. Although you don't possess the raw genius of giants in the field like Von Krumpf and Venkataraman, with access to centuries worth of texts, you eventually become a brilliant chronologist in your own right.

You discover that when you traveled forward from August 12, 2271, you somehow entered a pocket dimension—a leftover echo of a timestream that no longer exists. In fact, you can't even be sure there *is* a normal timestream remaining after the catastrophic event of 2271. Alas, by the time you've pieced together this puzzle, your time traveling days are long behind you.

Your crowning chronological achievement is to salvage a sliver of the Great Consciousness of the Persistent Universe that you find in the custodians' systems and house it in a small time machine (which you build into a gold watch because it seems like a cool thing to do). You're unable to test it yourself since it's only designed to transport someone who isn't peeled off the space-time continuum. But with the consciousness at its center, it can locate worthy adventurers and travel the timestream for eternity, righting wrongs throughout history.

You release your invention into the multiverse and die content.

THE END

You swear allegiance, and Fleck just about has a conniption fit. "Just sit tight," you whisper. "This royal magician thing might be important. I'll find you afterward!"

Armored guards escort you through the castle to a small room stuffed with glass beakers and various contraptions of indecipherable purpose. A man in a blue robe embroidered with stars and moons is examining a large vial filled with purple mist. His beard has grown longer, and he's really gone overboard with the medieval wizard look, but you'd recognize that wild-eyed gaze anywhere. It's the mad scientist!

He clearly recognizes you as well. "Seize the Dragon Knight!" he says. The guards quickly restrain you, and Nutso McCrazypants yanks your defunct time bracelet from your wrist.

"Six years I've wasted, trying to rebuild my broken time machine! The goblin hordes think they can leave me stranded in darkness, but then, YOU arrive! Just when I've solved the power conundrum? It's providence!" He shatters his vial, and you watch the mist coalesce around your time bracelet. Cackling, the scientist pushes a button on the device and steps into a time portal that opens between you.

Spooked, your captors loosen their grip. This is your chance to stop that guy from destroying history! Not to mention your only hope of ever leaving this horrible century. For the briefest moment, though, you hesitate. If you disappear now, what happens to Boris and Fleck? You did sort of promise them you'd help with that whole yoke of tyranny business.

▶ *If you escape through the portal while you can,*
   turn to page 236.

▶ *If you stay to help your friends,* **turn to page 161.**

You twist and turn and—just before they can grab you—get your tail through one of the rifts. As you do, something latches on and pulls you to the other side. Nice!

Wait a minute. Frick. It's more interdimensional time goblins.

You find yourself on a barren hillside. Off in the distance, you see some kind of shimmering dome and what might be a city inside it. Alas, between you and it are somehow even more goblins than you left behind in the void. A friggin' *ocean* of the things. They sweep in, completely surrounding you.

Then they open their mouths and, with a single voice, speak.

The noise almost deafens you. "2271?" They stare, transfixed, reading the tachyon particles floating off you like a book. "WHAT HAPPENS IN 2271? WE MUST SEND A SCOUTING PARTY TO 2271." Son of a bitch. Did you just *tip them off*? Before you can learn more, they attack. You're instantly crushed under the goblin wave.

I *told you* all these endings sucked.

THE END

You have a sudden billy club flashback and quickly decide that trusting your enigmatic neighbor is worth the risk. The moment you pass your arm through the bars, your wristband slips off. Well, that was easy. But was it smart?

"Back away from the rear wall," the voice says. "If my guess-work holds, this'll carve a hole just big enough to—"

A massive explosion knocks you off your feet. When the dust clears, you note that most of your cell's outside wall has been blown into the street along with a good portion of the one separating the two chambers. A small woman in a corset and goggles is hunched over in glee.

"Yeeheehee!" she says. "Come on, then! No time to dally!"

The woman darts off, and you follow, not knowing what else to do. She's much faster than you would guess based on her size, and you trail her eight or ten blocks—seriously, girl, *slow down*—into what must be the city's industrial quarter. It's raining again, and now you're soaked to the bone. She stops at the door of a dilapidated brick building and is engaged in a complicated series of knocks when you finally catch up to her.

(continue to the next page)

"Damnit, Cartwright!" she says. "It's me! Open the bloody door!"

The door swings open, and she pulls you inside. "Well, you're a funny looking one, aren't you," she says as you catch your breath, dripping on the wooden floor. "Still, you got me out of a tight spot, and anyone who winds up in that particular jail is likely a friend of mine." She holds out one hand. "Annabelle Biggers Shaughnessy," she says, "Gizmologist Extraordinaire. But you can call me Annie."

"*Gearbox* Annie," someone says from behind her. "For goodness' sake, take a towel, both of you, before you catch your death of cold." The voice belongs to an elegantly dressed gentleman in a top hat and waistcoat. His skin is a bit darker than Annie's, and he has a pointy little mustache.

"That's Professor Shankar Venkata-something-or-other," Annie says. "None of us can pronounce his name, so we just call him Bobbins. He's hoping that, once we free New Chicago from the grip of tyranny, we'll turn our attentions to his homeland."

"It's only British imperialism I object to, you understand," he says, "not their customs. Personally, I couldn't be happier to have been brought up in the industrialized world."

"Over there is my right-hand gal Cartwright and the Powder Monkeys, Pippa and Skip." Annie gestures toward a tall, broad woman in a grease-stained shirt and heavy gloves. Next to her are two children that you recognize from your altercation with the clockwork police officer earlier.

"We found them wandering the streets one day," Annie continues. "They don't say much, but I've never seen anyone better with explosives than the pair of them."

(continue to the next page)

This gives you pause. "They *are* terrorist eight-year-old children," you say.

Annie just laughs. "I suppose you could use that term to describe the lot of us. They call us the Gas Can Rebellion, although we only ever used gas cans to blow anything up that once. And don't you worry—we're much more discriminating than our reputation would suggest. I'm proud to report that, to date, our civilian casualty count stands at zero."

She explains that a pair of aristocratic sisters with access to incredibly advanced technology seized control of the city several years ago and have been ruling it with an iron fist ever since. Annie's little band of rebels is the only thing standing between them and the expansion of their empire to all of Northern Illinois (and from there, presumably, the world).

"Oh, I almost forgot," Annie says when she's finished her spiel. "This, of course, is yours."

She tosses you your time bracelet, which still has the dampener doohickey firmly attached. "I'll be honest with you," she says, "that thing isn't coming off without the key, which you'll only find on a chain around the necks of the wicked witches themselves. Without that, I'm afraid you'll find it useless."

She flashes you a devious grin. "However, your little gizmo is leaking aether like *crazy*. I've never seen anything like it. With that much juice, we could put an end to the sisters' tyranny once and for all. What do you say? Care to join our little organization?"

▶ *Heck yeah, you do! If the Gas Can Rebellion sounds like your idea of a good time,* **turn to page 203.**

▶ *Heck no, you don't. If the Gas Can Rebellion sounds like a surefire way to get yourself killed,* **turn to page 128.**

If this other entity is attempting to calm the ravenous prehistoric beast, it's probably a good idea to help it achieve that goal. You combine efforts and are surprised at how familiar the foreign consciousness seems. In fact, the moment you decide to treat it as a potential friend rather than a foe, you feel your minds begin to merge. Suddenly you realize that this isn't a foreign entity at all.

It's another version of you from an alternate timeline.

The two of you lived identical lives right up until that fateful moment when you witnessed the scientist murder his doppelganger. Then one of you returned to headquarters, peeled yourself off of the space-time continuum, jumped forward to 2271, had an audience with the living personification of the Persistent Universe, met Krikri the dolphin woman, escaped the clutches of interdimensional time goblins, traveled past the date from which no TTIA agent had ever returned, uncovered the mad scientist's entire life history, and tracked him here.

The other one followed the scientist through the portal, wound up inhabiting a T. rex, and benevolently decided not to eat the guy. So, in terms of recent experience, it's basically a tie? We're not here to pick favorites. Oh, also, one is from a universe where people evolved from dinosaurs, and the other is descended from mammals. Other than that, though, you're pretty much identical in every way.

The merging of two versions of the same mind gives you a laser-like focus that you've never experienced before. Seriously, you feel AMAZING. You immediately bend the primitive tyrannosaur to your will and settle into its massive form like a cozy winter coat.

(continue to the next page)

"Quick," Krikri says as you get your bearings. "Von Krumpf ran off this way!"

That's right—you're still trying to reconcile two completely different short term memories, but half of you knew that the mad scientist's name is Hercule Von Krumpf and that he's on a mission to rescue the love of his life who disappeared into a changing universe the moment they co-invented time travel.

As you follow Krikri into the forest, a column of blue light erupts into the sky from somewhere over the treeline. What the *what*? It pulsates into the clouds for a minute or two and then stops as mysteriously as it began. You hurry through the trees to investigate, and discover a clearing full of tents and other makeshift shelters.

The mad scientist is there, but he isn't alone. Several hundred additional Hercule Von Krumpfs are milling about and making adjustments to various pieces of scientific equipment. In the center of the encampment is a towering steel structure that dwarfs even your magnificent dinosaur form. "He just got here!" you exclaim. (The part of you from the dino-universe manages to contort your prehistoric vocal cords into a passable imitation of the English language, resulting in a voice much rougher and huskier than you're accustomed to, which you have to admit sounds pretty badass.) "Where did all this stuff come from?"

"He's doubling up," Krikri says. "Using this moment as a focal point and having versions of himself from different points in history converge here. If he's learned any of the tricks we did back in 2271, he could be pulling in alternate universe doppelgangers as well. Some of them must have traveled back further

(continue to the next page)

in time to begin construction on that... *thing*."

Whatever Von Krumpf's plan is, you're sure it hinges on the tower. But wait—if he succeeds, does that mean human beings will evolve from primates or from dinosaurs? You're losing track. Also, you've got memories from both timelines, so you're not even sure which one you're supposed to be protecting anymore. Ugh. Just thinking about it all is starting to hurt your brain.

The assembly of science clones, however, isn't going to wait for you to get your head on straight. One of them spots you on the edge of their clearing and shouts out an alarm. Soon they're everywhere, some rushing from the camp and others popping out of the forest behind you. They're a big, crazy-eyed mess, each with a spittle-flecked beard and a mass of machinery strapped to his chest. (If you ever need 300 jury-rigged, diesel-powered time machines, you know where to go.) Before you can react, one grabs Krikri by the arm. You roar in protest and tense up.

"Wait!" she says. "Everyone just calm down! I'm certain we can resolve this without resorting to violence!"

▶ *If you think Krikri's right and try talking things out with the nutters,* **turn to page 106.**

▶ *If you stick with your first instinct and rampage,* **turn to page 65.**

Honesty is the best policy, right? You lay out everything the Persistent Universe told you, as close to verbatim as you can recall. Frankly, you don't know enough about whatever goes through that woman's head to even *guess* what kind of B.S. might convince her that you're on the level.

When you finish, she just stares at you, her face slowly turning a deep crimson. Then, she taps you with her baton, disabling your personal gravity field. You float helplessly into the air.

"But… wait!" She taps you again, this time on the neck, and your vocal cords become as useless as your thrashing about. One of her subordinates escorts you (and by "escorts," we mean "pokes and prods you with a stick while you flail around wildly") into a room marked "storage." Inside are thousands of pods the size of refrigerators, including an entire wing labeled "Time Travel Investigation Agency." At least now you know what's been happening to all those agents trying to travel past 2271.

You're routed to a larger section, marked "Human-Sized Talking Dinosaurs." The Temporal Custodians freeze you in time and, without your help, don't even manage to *acknowledge* the massive, evil plot against them until it succeeds in wiping them out, along with every single living thing in the history of forever.

So that isn't great.

The End

Rocketing through the air while tied to a rickety, steam-powered projectile is the most terrifying thing you've ever experienced, and you're 95% sure you're about to die while you're doing it.

But you don't! Somehow, the rocket makes a beeline for a giant, scary-looking blimp floating above the clouds. Just as it's about to strike, Chance cuts your straps with a knife he's been holding between his teeth and leaps into an open hatch, pulling you along with him. There's a muffled explosion as the missile crashes against the blimp's armored hide, and the two of you skid across the floor safely.

Your partner bounces to his feet, dusting himself off. "That's why they call me *Chance*," he says. "'Because I always *take one*.'"

You're pretty shaken up from the ordeal. "How could that POSSIBLY have worked?"

Chance takes your tiny dinosaur hand in his big primate paw and helps you to your feet. "Remember the cookie thing?" he asks.

"Yeah, whenever you make a choice, it splits the timeline. So?"

"So any time a decision presents itself, I just choose randomly. That way, whichever version of me survives can come back in time and tell me the right way to go."

"OH MY GOD." Your brain is reeling with the implications. "How many timelines are there where we ROCKETED TO OUR DEATH out there, Chance?"

He shrugs. "Hundreds? Thousands? What does it matter? Only the one that lived could have come back to aim the missile for us. See? It's foolproof!"

(continue to the next page)

You're pretty sure there's a flaw in his logic somewhere, but your partner has already moved on and is peeking through a doorway into a huge chamber bustling with activity. "There's the dark-haired sister up on that catwalk," he says, pointing. "The blonde is on the far side of the room. Let's see…" He pauses, silently tilting his head back and forth the slightest bit.

"Chance, are you doing *eenie-meenie-miney-moe*? Because that's not random! It has a very specific outcome based on the number of syllables in—"

"Blonde!" he says, launching himself into the chamber. "You stop the brunette! Go forth and *thwart*, my friend!"

You look through the doorway and see your target perched up on a walkway near a weird, glowing orb. There's a ladder attached to the room's central column, which is far from ideal, since your arms are pretty much useless for that sort of thing. What concerns you even more, though, are the dozens of lackeys and eight-foot-tall steampunk robots milling about between you and it. You scan the room for an alternate route and spot a second ladder on a wall that should be a little easier to get to, if no easier to climb.

Along the opposite wall, you're surprised to see another dino-person peeking hesitantly through another doorway. Even from this distance, you're pretty sure it's an alternate-timeline version of yourself. What are *you* doing here?

▶ *If you stick to the plan and go after your designated steampunk crime boss,* **turn to page 284.**

▶ *If you make your way toward the doppelganger, hoping to combine efforts,* **turn to page 196.**

"That's actually what I was trying to do when you showed up," you say. "But I couldn't quite bring myself to pull the trigger."

"Ah, but if you want to travel through time, you must," Bruxelles says. "Otherwise, when the universe changes around you, you change too. Or just disappear. Poof."

"That's what I've been saying," Professor V. says.

"But you only went back one minute," Bruxelles says. "Of course you don't want to kill yourself like that, it's like looking in a mirror!" He hops on his motorcycle, and holds out one hand for you to join him. "Here, we'll do this the easy way."

The easy way sounds good to you. You squeeze yourself onto the seat behind him as he punches numbers into a computer console on his handlebars. After a bright flash and a brief laser light show, you find yourself in your own bedroom with the lights out. Lying in bed in front of you, fast asleep, is yourself.

"Now take all the time that you need," Bruxelles says. "Just don't wake yourself up, and it's a piece of cake."

A piece of cake? "If anything, this is worse! I can't murder myself in my sleep!"

"Well, if you want, I suppose I can do it for you."

"You can? Really?"

"Of course," he says, pulling his gun out of his holster. "I shoot people all the time, no problem."

"No, I mean does it work like that? If you kill me, does it still make a paradox and peel me off the space-time continuum?"

"Oh." He tilts his head, thinking. "I'm not sure. To tell you the truth, none of this stuff makes a whole lot of sense to me."

▶ *If you let Bruxelles pull the trigger,* **turn to page 136.**

▶ *If you're pretty sure this is something you need to do for yourself,* **turn to page 57.**

As much as you've been enjoying your time with the Freakporium—seriously, those guys seem *super* cool—being trapped in the Middle Ages isn't helping you track down any mad scientists or repair any timelines. Also, if there *is* a real dragon, you're not sure what Crabbe thinks you can do about it. You bid him farewell and good luck.

The jumpsuit woman generates another portal, and you enter it together. On the other side, you find yourself in the moonbase of the Temporal Custodians of the Persistent Universe. Or, technically, in their remote training facility, as their main building has been completely overrun. The chamber is filled with shimmering portals and time travelers of all descriptions stepping out of them.

"I'm not sure if you're one of the alternates I've met already," the woman says, "but I'm Velox, leader of what remains of the Temporal Custodians."

You're getting the impression that the fight against the interdimensional time goblins has not been going particularly well. Perhaps you should have taken your chances with the dragon instead?

"We're organizing into regiments," Velox says. "Come this way. I've got just the detachment for you."

▶ Turn to page 222.

"This," you say, "looks like a job for *Thunder Lizard*."

Instead of the gun, Cartwright gives you something she calls a shock rod. You're not a hundred percent sure what it does, but you leap into the room and let out a wail that, back home, would sound goofy and forced. To the primates of 1882, though, it's the roar of a freaking Tyrannosaurus rex.

They totally lose their marbles.

The ensuing chaos provides Cartwright all the opportunity she needs to shoot the snipers out of their perch—they hit the floor before you even finish vocalizing. You dive behind a stack of crates before the yokels gather their wits and open fire. Alas, the clockwork centurions don't seem as intimidated by your display of dino-terror, and one of them lumbers toward you. "Warning, citizen! Surrender or suffer the full force of—" You smack it with your stick, which emits a burst of electricity on impact. The automaton emits a screech and falls in a heap to the floor.

So *that's* what a shock rod does. Nice.

You peek around a crate to witness a scene of utter insanity. Lackeys fire weapons throughout the cabin seemingly at random—maybe not the most brilliant plan on a hydrogen-filled airship, no matter how sturdily constructed?—and their clockwork compatriots are milling about in confusion, pretty much asking to be immobilized by your electric pig sticker. Annie is quietly pulling wires out from an open console, and Bobbins is inching slowly toward his designated station.

Before he gets there, he's tackled by one of the men you saw at the terminals earlier. "You! But how—" You're not even sure which one of them makes the exclamation—other than a few

(continue to the next page)

extra pounds and a touch more facial hair, the second man is the spitting image of your crewmember. Uh oh. More time travel shenanigans? Or is it possible that they're simply brothers? Not every evil twin is necessarily the result of meddling in the space-time—

Before you can finish speculating, a stray bullet hits one of the Powder Monkeys' emergency charges, blasting a hole clear through the cabin's exterior wall and sucking both men right out into the night sky.

"Nooooo!" Cartwright screams, then howls a second time as she takes a hit to the shoulder.

"Somebody get to the switch!" Annie yells from across the room. "I've just about got this—"

There's a loud smack, and she stops abruptly mid-sentence. You break into a sprint toward the switch, ready to take over for your fallen companion, and see Annie slumped on the floor with Cornelia standing over her, a shock rod just like yours in her hands.

"My dear Annabelle," she says. "You should have stayed in the attic where you belong."

Bobbins is gone. Cartwright is down. Annie is unconscious. Did she manage to finish her task? If you pull the switch now, it might make the engines seize up and send the ship into a tailspin, just as planned. Or it might just turn on the damn glowing orb, whatever the hell it even is. Should you risk it? You haven't seen the Powder Monkeys since this madness started. Maybe you should just get out of there and hope plan B works out?

▶ *If you pull the switch,* **turn to page 184.**

▶ *If you run like hell and try to make it to an orntithoptivelocipede,* **turn to page 237.**

What the hell. "I AM THE LORD OF ALL DRAGONS," you say in your deepest, scariest growl. "Drop your weapon, or suffer the wrath of my mighty talons! And firebreathing! And whatnot!"

It's a pretty good showing, and the townsfolk cower like nobody's business. The knight, however, is made of sterner stuff. His blade flashes out, and before you can switch tactics and reconsider the whole begging-for-mercy angle, it's all over. Afterward, your head is mounted on a pike and paraded all over the countryside in celebration of Lord Fenwick, the Dragon Slayer. Throughout his life, it remains his most valued possession, and when historians eventually dig the skull of a miniaturized, adult T. rex out of his long-buried treasure room, it sends them into conniption fits.

You singlehandedly set the science of archeology back decades.

You snatch that crazy bastard up in your massive jaws and swallow him whole, time machine and all. Ew. Even as an indiscriminate hunter and scavenger who devours everything from fresh Triceratops to month-old carrion, this guy tastes *awful*. Also, the act of savagery brings your tyrannosaurish instincts to the fore, overwhelming the fragile control you've established over your host body.

Forget everything we said about being a human being. YOU ARE T. REX, UNDISPUTED MONARCH OF THE CRETACEOUS. You let out a mighty roar that shakes the foliage and sends a nearby pterosaur flapping into the sky.

As you do, there's an uncomfortable twinge in your belly, and an enormous, shimmering hole in space-time appears in thin air before you. Whoa. Did you just belch up a *time portal*? It sits there, beckoning you to enter. Do you even want to, though? Seriously, what else in all of history could possibly beat *this*?

▶ *If you hop through the portal,* **turn to page 144.**

▶ *If you're happy calling the Cretaceous your home,* **turn to page 88.**

The world starts spinning around you again, and you find yourself back in the familiar confines of Professor V.'s lab. You look down at your appendages and are pleased to see small, reptilian claws. You're a human-sized dinosaur again!

Human-sized dinosaur? That's a weird way to put it. You're a tyrannoid, like you've always been. Why would you expect anything different? You notice a door in the back of the lab that you've never seen before. It's cracked open, and you can hear voices coming from inside.

"I got it after we crash-landed on the moon in 2271," a woman says in gentle, melodious tones. "Sadly, I'm afraid your assistant will be stranded there forever."

You hear Professor Velociraptor sigh. Wait. *You're* Professor V.'s assistant. Did that woman just say you were stranded forever? *On the moon?*

"I need to generate a portal in order to bring an alternate version of you to the Cretaceous period," the mysterious woman continues. "It's kind of a long story. Can you fix it?"

You're so absorbed in your eavesdropping that you almost don't notice the jagged purple rift in space-time open up in the middle of the room behind you. *Almost.* Two creepy, gnarled creatures emerge from the crack, run straight for the Bakulan time travel rig, and start hitting it with their gross little fists. Hey! That's a sensitive piece of equipment! Also, if they wreck it, you're probably out of a job.

▶ *If you rush to the back room to warn Professor V. of the attack,* **turn to page 157.**

▶ *If you try to stop the creatures yourself before they can do any more damage,* **turn to page 35.**

You decide to lay your cards on the table so your alternate self can at least make an informed decision. "I might be the wrong person to ask," you say. "Professor V. sent me here, and I've just kind of been tagging along with this guy all day."

Regular Chance explains his missile plan to Past Chance and gets ready to aim the terrifying contraption at some unspecified point above the clouds while his double ties one arm to it with a rope. Your own doppelganger, on the other hand, looks dubious as all hell and, after a bit of hemming and hawing, finally decides against making the trip.

"Surely we can find a way to get to that airship that *isn't* completely and utterly insane."

Past Chance unties himself dejectedly, and the two of them march off down the street, discussing their options.

Regular Chance looks sad. "But… we took the *missile*," he says. "Oh well, no matter. We have a motorcycle to find! I'm sure everything will work itself out in the end."

The thing is, it doesn't. It turns out the Steampunk Mafia's nefarious scheme involves a really, *really* big explosion—really, *really* soon. And that missile was your only hope to get there in time to prevent it. Five minutes later, without warning, you're completely atomized, along with your double, both versions of Chance, all of New Chicago, and really the bulk of the North American Continent.

It's quite something, really.

THE END

Even if it isn't functioning at quite a hundred percent, you have a freaking *time machine*. There's no way you're going to splatter yourself all over the inside of some spacecraft without at least *trying* to use it. You jump into the wretched demi-portal.

… And immediately regret the decision. Every iota of your being explodes in pain as your consciousness is ripped out of your physical form. It turns out this portal isn't stable enough to transport physical matter (it's a *really* crappy portal) and leaves your body behind, hurling your awareness back through the timestream Bakula-style.

The experience is quite jarring. In fact, when you eventually find yourself on stable ground, your memory is all but shattered. Did you come here from… *some kind of UFO*? Or… *the moon*? That can't be right. What you know for sure is that you work for the Time Travel Investigation Agency, and you're weirdly preoccupied with the three unbreakable laws of time travel. Wait, those things *are* unbreakable, aren't they? Suddenly you're not so sure.

We should also mention that you're in the body of a Labrador retriever, watching a bearded maniac kill his alternate self and jump into a time portal on the other side of the room. Before you can get your bearings, the part of your mind that *didn't* just experience traumatic psychic brain injury makes a quick judgement call and decides to leap in after him.

▶ **Turn to page 7.**

There's a ladder here on the central column, and you half-slide, half-fall down it at top speed. Your landing is quite painful, and you twist up your ankle pretty severely in the process. Fortunately, you discover the switch box mounted at the base of the column, so you don't even *need* that ankle. You flip the big, oversized lever from the clearly labeled "on" position to "off," and...

Nothing happens.

The ship's engines originally lit the disco ball's fuse, but at this point, it's drawing energy from the *multiverse itself*. It blows before you can even consider a last-ditch escape plan. Which would have been irrelevant anyway because, if anything, Beatrice was *underselling* it. The blast takes out not just the airship, or New Chicago, or the midwestern United States. All of North America is incinerated instantly, and the resulting atmospheric catastrophe kills every living thing on the planet within days.

Because you stopped the sisters from completing their plan, however, at least the global extinction is limited to a single timestream. I mean, it's not like you're getting a medal for that or anything. But it's definitely not the *worst* ending in this book.

The End

Really? Wow. That's awfully noble of you. And it's probably for the best because someone has to save the universe from certain destruction, and all this screwing around trying to get on with it isn't doing the space-time continuum any favors.

Your alternate self finally works up the courage to finish the job and then goes on to have all sorts of adventures in every corner of time and space. Stopping the asteroid that killed off your dinosaur ancestors. Meeting a talking dolphin. Uncovering the deepest secrets of the mysterious Persistent Universe. You should be proud that your selfless sacrifice has allowed another version of yourself to accomplish so many wonderful things.

That's your double, though. All you manage to do is get yourself shot. In the face.

WHY DOES IT ALWAYS HAVE TO BE THE FACE?

THE END

You're not sure what's going on here, but it occurs to you that a prehistoric T. rex in the Middle Ages probably means time travel shenanigans of one kind or another. If that thing somehow got to this century, perhaps it could lead you to a way out? The local townsfolk claim that it makes its home in the hills, so you set off to investigate.

You wander for a couple of hours but don't have much luck locating dinosaur tracks. As you crest a gentle, grassy slope, however, you hear a shout from somewhere behind you.

"Draaaaaaagon!" You turn around, but all you see is an armored man on horseback, apparently doing the shouting.

You wave and shout back at him. "Wheeeeeeere?"

He spurs his horse toward you, which is nice because you'd rather not have this entire conversation at the top of your lungs. He closes the distance between you rapidly—wow, that horse can really move. Just when you expect him to slow down, however, he snaps his helmet's visor shut and lowers a big, pointy stick.

Hold on. Does this guy think *you're* the—

The horseman crashes into you before you can finish your thought, impaling you on his lance. "For king and country, have at thee, vile creature!" he yells. "You shall terrorize my kinsmen no more!"

You get slain on a field of valor you *didn't even know you were on*. The Middle Ages, it turns out, kind of suck.

THE END

Very little of what's happened today makes much sense if you pause to think about it. But you're sure of approximately two things: Krikri is perfectly capable of taking care of herself and that God damn mechanical dinosaur isn't going to wreck any giant laser towers if *you* have anything to say about it.

Of course, you really don't. You can't hope to defeat it head-to-head. But you'll settle for distracting it long enough for Von Krumpf to do whatever it is he's doing. So you bluff. It isn't a *spectacular* plan—particularly considering you're almost certainly throwing your life away by executing it—but it's what you've got. You charge toward the robosaur head first, then plant your feet right in its path and let out an ear-splitting roar as if *it's* the thing that should be terrified of *you*.

It works! The robot screeches to a halt and roars back, sizing you up. Before it has the chance to come to any conclusions, though, you lunge at its throat, and it swiftly dodges away. It's a good thing, too, because you're pretty sure you would have broken your teeth on the damn thing. You circle each other for a few moments, but there's only so far bravado can carry you. It finishes its analysis of your abilities, finds them wanting, and attacks. Alas, you're nowhere near quick enough to get out of its way.

Well, crud. Throwing your life away didn't buy you nearly as much time as you'd hoped.

Just as your ass is *milliseconds* from being grass, the tower explodes to life behind you, drawing your adversary's attention away from your tender fleshy bits. Saved by the beam! Which, by the way, is blinding purple now and crackling with what you hope is enough power to wipe out an incoming comet.

(continue to the next page)

Fortunately, it is! The initial, comet-smashing blast, however, is only a prelude to the main event. The beam's spectrum shifts from purple to white and, with a concussive blast that knocks over everything in the immediate vicinity weighing less than a ton, reverses polarity. Instead of pumping energy out into the cosmos, it now appears to be *pulling energy in*.

The good news is, the blast was an electromagnetic pulse, which completely fries the robosaur's circuitry and renders it inert. The bad news is that it also shorts out Professor V's equipment. Once again, the tachyon shield sputters and fizzles out. Rather than renewing their attack, though, the goblins turn tail and run, sprinting for any rifts close enough to the ground to scamper into. You take one look at the tower, now glowing white-hot like the sun and can guess why.

What the devil is Von Krumpf up to? Is it possible that he's still as nutty as squirrel poo and the whole merging alternate selves business just made him three hundred times better at hiding it? No, surely you can trust him. Besides, what's the alternative?

Sigh. Sacrificing yourself to save all of freakin' creation is beginning to get old.

▶ *If you think this new development means Von Krumpf if trying to destroy the multiverse, and you hurl yourself at the tower in a desperate attempt to stop him,* **turn to page 175.**

▶ *If you're pretty sure Von Krumpf is okay, and you assume whatever he's doing is pro-multiverse,* **turn to page 288.**

You promised Professor V. that you'd safeguard the time-line, and you'll be damned if you're going to let something trivial like being stranded in a deserted urban wasteland get in the way. Before long, Krikri's modifications are complete, and you're strapped into the newly upgraded time machine, cross-Bakulating into whatever alternate past Hercule Von Krumpf originated in. The first thing you discover, to your relief, is that Betsy remains unchanged in this reality, waiting to be your faithful observation deck.

The second thing you discover is that Von Krumpf was a *dinosaur*.

A Triceratops, to be exact, just as disheveled as ever but far less crazy-eyed. In fact, he looks almost distinguished now that you see him as a regular dino-person rather than the hairy-faced mammal with flecks of spittle in his beard. You and Krikri resume your research and uncover a very different story this time around.

Although his early life followed much the same path, Von Krumpf seems a bit more cheerful and less withdrawn. After inventing Bakulan time travel in 1955, he continued to tinker with the technology over the following decades. Then in 1983, he met a dapper Canadian Parasaurolophus mathematician named Desmond and came to trust him enough to share his research. The two men began working together, and one day after a time travel session, Desmond walked straight to Von Krumpf and embraced him in a deeply passionate kiss.

"Wow," you say after returning from the past with this latest bit of information. "I *did not* see that coming."

"How could you *miss* it?" Krikri says. "The unspoken

(continue to the next page)

passion between them has been brewing for *months!*"

"Um, I guess I thought they just respected each other as scientists? Plus, Von Krumpf didn't give me a gay vibe at all."

"Pft," she says. "People don't have to be just one thing. And anyway, sometimes someone is so perfect for you that none of that other stuff even matters."

You continue your observations (after Krikri goes back to witness that first kiss herself and point out various subtleties that you were completely oblivious to). You discover that it was Desmond who first theorized the possibility of non-Bakulan time travel and Von Krumpf who conceptualized an entirely new field of mathematics to make it a reality. After months

(continue to the next page)

of working together on the project, they threw the switch of their new space-time wormhole portal generator together, hand-in-hand.

And completely shattered the fabric of the universe.

Whatever chain of events was set in motion from introducing physical time travel to the world meant that dinosaurs went extinct, human beings evolved from monkeys instead, and a huge number of people never properly existed at all, Desmond among them. Von Krumpf, however, could still remember the original timeline. It's possible that he was compelled to re-invent the device by a universe attempting to self-correct its own paradox. Or, as Krikri speculates, he may have just kept the image of his true love in his mind and worked through all the madness brought upon by a changing reality until he built the one tool capable of bringing him back. One way or the other, Von Krumpf invented non-Bakulan time travel once again, from scratch, which is where you first crossed paths with him.

"He's trying to fix his own timeline and bring Desmond back," Krikri says. "That *has* to be it. Now, all we have to do is find out where he went on that first jump and be there to meet him."

"So I Bakulate into Betsy, follow him through the portal, and report back," you say. "Done and done."

"I'm worried that going through a physical portal might break your connection to the present and leave you stranded wherever you end up," Krikri says. "It's safer if I use my own device to seek him out in the timestream. I can pinpoint spikes in temporal activity like your professor did, so I won't be searching blind."

(continue to the next page)

It dawns on you that if Von Krumpf is trying to fix his own timeline, it's the one where people evolved from dinosaurs. It's *your* timeline. And if monkey people are wandering around on that moonbase you escaped from, it's because he failed in his effort, not because he succeeded.

Even though you've come to rely on Krikri and respect her as much as is dinosaurily possible, ultimately, you each have your own horse in this race. You can either wind up in a universe where people evolved from dinosaurs or dolphins, not both. You hate the very idea that you and your friend are working at cross-purposes. But even if she's right and you get stuck somewhere in the past with Von Krumpf, perhaps it's time that you and Krikri part ways.

▶ *If you go with your original idea and make one last time jump into the Labrador retriever,* **turn to page 46.**

▶ *If you throw your lot in with Krikri and trust her to find Von Krumpf,* **turn to page 194.**

Seriously, how are *you* supposed to know which bomb to use? For just a moment, you ponder the utter unjustness of being presented with a potentially life-or-death decision while having very little in the way of relevant information. Then you take a stab in the dark.

"CONCUSSIVE!" you yell back to your passenger.

It doesn't work *for crap*. Skip chucks a pair of smallish, spiky-looking things into the open hatch, and you're immediately treated to an explosion which would probably be deafening if you could hear anything from your open-air-bicycle seat anyway. Black smoke wafts out of the opening. Looks good so far, right?

Alas, your luck doesn't hold. A huge, automated gun turret lowers from the ship's undercarriage and opens fire on you. From this range, it doesn't take much in the way of ordnance to rip the ornithoptivelocipede's wings to shreds. The Powder Monkey leaps from his perch behind you in a desperate attempt to grab onto the airship, or an enemy craft, or anything that isn't a useless, plummeting death-trap.

You, of course, are still carefully tied to it when it hits the ground.

THE END

Seriously?

▶ *Nah, just kidding. If you open fire,* **turn to page 147.**

▶ *Or, if you honestly think you've figured out a way to end this without bloodshed,* **turn to page 89.**

You tell Bruxelles to chill, but he's having none of it. "If it were one or two duplicates, maybe," he says. "But all this? Every second causes more stress on the continuum. So unless you have a way to smoosh all these jokers back together—"

"That's it!" Hercule exclaims. "I fell into the beam! It combined two versions of me from separate timelines, and for just a moment, I could *think*." That does make a certain amount of sense—when your dinosaur self and your mammal self combined, your brain felt like a million bucks.

"If I merge with the rest of the duplicates, maybe I can…" he trails off, then grunts in frustration, banging his head with the palm of his hand. "Please, I know this will work!"

Krikri fully supports his plan, and Bruxelles grudgingly agrees. You follow the sea of Von Krumpfs into the tower and watch as they fiddle with dials and throw switches on the walls of the large, central chamber. The entire structure turns out to be some kind of tachyon-powered laser, which explains the column of light you witnessed earlier. After a few minutes of preparation, the massive blue beam erupts from a pit in the middle of the room. One of the science clones clenches his teeth and slowly steps into it.

His body—clothing, time travel chest rig, and all—utterly disintegrates. "It's working!" Hercule gasps. "I just stepped in, then I was… here!" One by one, the rest of the doppelgangers follow suit. Hercule grows more excited, and more focused, with each one. "Of course! I built this machine to bring back Desmond but lost sight of the reason I traveled here in the first place. The comet! They're going to hurl a comet at us. That's what changes the timestream to begin with!"

(continue to the next page)

Krikri's soulful little dolphin eyes widen. "What? *Who's* going to hurl a comet at us?"

"Interdimensional time goblins!"

Bruxelles rushes toward the entryway, crashing into a pair of gnarled, vaguely humanoid figures and expelling them from the room with a roundhouse kick. You hurry to his side and see dozens of the creepy little things amassing outside. There's a crack of thunder, and hundreds of additional goblins start pouring from jagged rifts that burst open in the clear blue sky.

"Too many!" Bruxelles says. "I have to get to my timecycle!"

Krikri, as always, remains calm. "What do they want?"

"We've never been able to find out," Bruxelles says. "They have no language we can decipher and don't respond to any form of communication. If there's a way inside their ugly little heads, we haven't found it."

A way inside their heads? Krikri seems to be thinking the same thing you are. "We can use the machine in 2271 and Bakulate into one of them!" she says.

"I'll go," you say.

Bruxelles is busy deflecting individual goblins as they throw themselves at the tower's entryway. He seems stressed. "Um, I think I could use the dinosaur's help fighting these things."

Fortunately, you can do both. Half of your mind is still tethered to 2271, but the other half was disconnected when you first jumped through that time portal. Leaving the Cretaceous period will simply split your consciousness back in two.

▶ *To follow the half of your brain traveling millions of years on a vital research mission,* **turn to page 165.**

▶ *To stay with the half in the past, helping Bruxelles battle interdimensional time goblins,* **turn to page 217.**

You select your cookie and pop the whole thing into your enormous dino-mouth. It's pretty tasty.

"And with that simple decision," Professor V. says, "you've split the timeline. Somewhere in the multiverse, there's an alternate version of you, right now, eating the other cookie."

"Ha!" Chance says. You note that he's chewing on the cookie you didn't pick. "I love the cookie thing! It's like, I never know in advance what cookie I'm going to get!"

You ignore him. "You know, a dinosaur version of you once told me that alternate timelines were impossible."

"Aha!" Professor V. says. "You must be one of my old students from the Time Travel Investigation Agency. I *thought* you seemed familiar. Those rules only ever applied to Bakulan time travel, though. We left all that behind a very long time ago."

Although you're technically in the year 2024, Time Patrol HQ actually exists frozen in a single millisecond, moving sideways through the spaces between alternate realities rather than forward in time. It's a lot to grasp, but Professor V. explains that she's been working here for more than two decades.

"Okay, okay," Chance says. "No bringing back civilians, eat the cookie, we live in a timeless pocket dimension. That's everything, right? We can go now?"

You're still trying to get your head around the concept of moving sideways through time. "What's the rush?"

"Your first mission," he says through a wide grin. "The Steampunk Mafia of 1882 has been importing illegal future tech, and we're going to stop them." You turn to say goodbye to the professor and are surprised to discover that she has the head of a Labrador retriever.

(continue to the next page)

Aaaaagh.

"Looking good, Professor V.!" Chance says, waving farewell. "That's nothing," he whispers as you leave. "One day, she had evolved from a tree. She spoke by rustling her leaves or something? I couldn't understand a single word."

He takes you to his timecycle—you'll be sharing one until your probationary period is up—and hops on, patting the seat behind him. After a quick ride through the timestream, you find yourself in a back alley, cobblestones beneath your tires wet from a recent downpour.

"Come on," your partner says, pushing down the bike's kickstand and dismounting in one fluid motion. "We've got lackeys and thugs to intimidate."

"Um, Chance?" You gesture at the motorcycle. "Is it safe to just leave this thing here?"

"Sure. Someone will come get it. When we're done with the mission, I file paperwork with the exact moment I left it and the exact moment I need it again, and one of our technicians moves it for me. It's super cool."

"But wouldn't that mean the technician should be here right now?" You look up and down the alley but see no technician.

"Yeah, sometimes I forget to file the paperwork," Chance says. "If you're worried about it, stay here with the bike. I'll be back in maybe twenty minutes. Half an hour, tops."

Without your armband, you're completely reliant on the timecycle if you ever want to leave the 1880s. Perhaps you should stay here and guard it?

▶ *If you go with Chance to beat up roustabouts or whatever he's planning to do,* **turn to page 5.**

▶ *If you stay with the time machine,* **turn to page 160.**

You're guessing that whatever "complete control over the fabric of reality itself" means, it has something to do with that glowing disco ball up in the rafters. You can visit with alternate universe versions of yourself *after* you've finished the job you came here to do. For now, it's *thwarting* time.

You scoot over to the second ladder and commence climbing, primarily with your legs and teeth. Progress is not terribly rapid, and you chip a couple of molars on the way up, but after a few minutes you reach the catwalk, only to discover a pair of thugs with scoped rifles lying in wait. (One of them, you're oddly pleased to note, is a *lady* thug.)

Just as they spot you, a terrible ruckus erupts from the floor below. You freeze as the snipers level their rifles at you, but before they can shoot, gunfire erupts from elsewhere in the chamber. Two precise shots hit the snipers in their respective temples and send them toppling over the railing.

Convenient! You hurry across the catwalk toward the room's center, where the dark-haired sister is crouched on the railing. The walkway doesn't reach all the way to the orb, which is mounted to the ceiling several feet away from her. She looks like she's preparing to jump.

"Step away from the, uh… glowy thing," you say in your best action-movie-hero tone, "and no one gets hurt."

"Ha!" Beatrice says. "Once my sister throws the switch, *you will be the one who is the hurt getter!*"

You feel better about your attempt at banter since Beatrice's is absolute rubbish. Also, you scan the chaos beneath you and, amid the screaming henchmen and confused-looking automatons, spot Cornelia slumped on the floor, likely the recipient of

(continue to the next page)

Chance's patented roundhouse kick.

"That sister? Face it, Beatrice. It's over. We've won."

Before you can ramp up your victory monologue, though, you hear a low thrumming sound. The orb flashes, pulsates, and grows slightly larger. Son of a bitch. Cornelia or no Cornelia, the chamber is filled with all manner of henchpeople who are capable of working a switch. Apparently, some asshole down there has gone and pulled it.

Beatrice squeals with glee. "Sorry, Cornelia dear. The infinite fabric of reality will have to do with a single human intellect it its core."

"Don't move!" More than a hint of desperation is creeping into that action-hero voice you were working on. "I swear to God, I'll knock you off this catwalk if I have to!"

"You're too late! With or without my intellect, this contraption is going off like a powder keg. The detonation will be... prodigious. Gargantuan. *Continental!*"

Beatrice jumps from of the railing, and you leap to intercept, spinning and knocking her away from the glowing sphere with your tail. Howling, she falls and hits the floor below with a thud.

The orb, however, continues to expand. It *does* look like it might explode. Surely she was exaggerating the magnitude of it, though. Considering your difficulty with ladders, you're not certain you can get to the power switch in time to shut things down. Nevertheless, it's your only hope.

Wait, though. What if *you* gained complete control over the fabric of reality?

▶ *If you haul ass for the power switch,* **turn to page 269.**

▶ *If you hurl yourself into the disco ball of doom,*
   turn to page 45.

The world starts spinning around you again, and you find yourself in the familiar confines of Professor V.'s lab. You look down at your appendages and see leafy branches. You're a human-sized pear tree!

Human-sized pear tree? That's a weird way to put it. You're a pyrusoid, like you've always been. Why would you expect anything different? You notice a door in the back of the lab that you've never seen before. It's cracked open, and you can hear voices coming from inside.

"An alternate version of you repaired it for me," a woman says in a truly bizarre accent. It's almost as if she's trying to emulate standard foliage-rustling with... a *dolphin mouth*?

Your boss, Professor Vegetatious, answers her. "And you want to modify the time tunnel to shield it from goblins? I'm afraid I don't have the expertise for that."

A jagged rift in space-time opens in the middle of the room, and two interdimensional time goblins hop through it and start attacking the professor's time machine. You know you should stop them, or at least warn Professor V., but some tiny voice inside you is screaming that *all of this is wrong*. That you've become unstuck from reality and are shifting from one dimension to another at random. That's *insane*, though, right? Surely you should ignore that voice and concentrate on the terrifying creatures that appeared out of nowhere.

▶ *If you rush to the back room to warn Professor V. about the goblins,* **turn to page 157.**

▶ *If you try to stop the creatures yourself,* **turn to page 35.**

▶ *If you freak out and start shrieking about alternate realities and the space-time continuum,* **turn to page 6.**

Even though the Geneva Conventions won't be passed for a least another 600 years, you're pretty sure assassinating world leaders is already wrong. Fortunately, Boris proves to be a truly inspiring public speaker. His revolutionary spirit is infectious, and within a week, you've raised an army of huddled masses from all across the countryside, actively yearning to be free.

Your 10,000 troops march on the castle and demand that the monarch step down. Said monarch, however, doesn't respond as you hoped. And *his* armies have armor, not to mention weapons that aren't normally used for farming mud.

Horns blow, and suddenly the royal cavalry descends from the surrounding hills, cutting through the peasant regiments like butter. It's a massacre.

Boris is mortified. "But… *the yoke of tyranny*," he mutters. He checks his timepiece and discovers that the light on top is blinking red. "What? That's never happened before. Could I have screwed this up so badly that—"

With a flash of light, Boris is gone. Hey! That guy was your ride!

Fleck comes running into your command tent. "The troops need orders, Your Gloriousness!"

So far the rebellion has been an unmitigated disaster. Should you give the command to surrender and save as many of your troops as possible? Or push on in hopes of salvaging some sort of victory?

▶ *If you give up,* **turn to page 212.**

▶ *If you fight until the last man,* **turn to page 109.**

With everything you've just gone through, that guy had BETTER not be trying to destroy the freaking multiverse. You rush toward the glowing tower but stop short of any desperate, hurling attempts. Because, you know, that thing looks *super* dangerous.

You carefully circle the structure, trying to discover what's going on inside without getting yourself fricasseed in the attempt. Your caution proves unnecessary, though—after a few

(continue to the next page)

moments, the tower powers down on its own. With the goblins beating a hasty retreat, Krikri and Bruxelles have come to investigate as well, and the three of you make your way inside. You see Professor V. intently studying a console and Von Krumpf helping someone out of the shallow pit built into the center of the room.

It's a well-dressed gentleman who appears to have evolved from a Parasaurolophus. He's the same size and roughly the same proportions as any human being, but has kept the facial features, finely-scaled skin, long neck and prominent forehead crest of his distant ancestors. He appears momentarily confused, then looks into Von Krumpf's eyes, gasps, and immediately sweeps the shorter man up in a long, passionate, dinosaur-on-primate kiss.

"Desmond," Von Krumpf says, eyes red. "I thought I'd lost you forever. I'm so sorry. I'm so, *so* sorry."

Desmond brushes the hair away from his partner's eyes and puts a hand on each cheek, drawing him close. "Lost me? Hercule, you *found* me. I always knew you would."

You turn to see tears streaming down Krikri's face, along with a smile that stretches from ear to ear (or, technically, from eye to eye—dolphin faces are kind of weird). Bruxelles is biting his lower lip and trying to hold back a sniffle. "It's because one of those goblins punched me in the face," he says, finally blowing his nose into his recovered shirt sleeve. "I'm not crying because of *feelings*."

Professor V. insists that you give the reunited lovers some privacy and joins you outside. "What now?" she asks after finally managing to pull Krikri away from the display of affection. "The

(continue to the next page)

EMP completely wrecked my time bracelet, and very little of the equipment inside appears salvageable. I'm afraid we may be stuck here."

"Hmm," Krikri says. "The mechanical components of my internal device seem to be fried as well."

Bruxelles seems unvexed. "No worries, my friends! A future version of me will be along to rescue us at any moment. This kind of thing happens to me all the time!" Professor V. tries to explain to him that if he never leaves the Cretaceous period there will never be a future, time traveling version of him to do any rescuing. But he's having none of it.

Krikri takes you aside. "You know what we did today, right?"

"Um, saved the entire freaking multiverse?"

"You bet your ass we did!" She gives you a big hug on your giant dino-thigh. "Now come help me take stock of the campsite." Her smile narrows just the tiniest bit.

"I have a feeling we might be here for a while."

THE END

There's something about these two that you don't trust. You decline their offer, as much as it pains you to do so.

"Alas and alack, the performing life is not for all," Crabbe says. "Fortunately, we operate another enterprise in addition to the Freakporium."

The little man grins, displaying a sparse collection of half-rotten teeth. "Toby and Crabbe's Exotic Meats," he says, drawing a wicked-looking curved blade from under his robe. "Crabbe, what do you suspect folks might pay for talking dragon steak?"

"One and twenty sixpence, if it's a ha'penny," the larger man says. His assessment of your value sounds like gibberish to you, but you have more pressing concerns. Before you can tell them you've changed your mind about breakfast, Toby's blade is at your throat. He slaughters you quickly and cleanly, so as not to damage any prime cuts.

Good instincts, by the way.

THE END

You hesitate to trust your aerial safety to a guy who just asked you if you think a missile "might explode." Infiltrating the Steampunk Mafia's secret bunker, on the other hand, proves surprisingly easy. Just around the corner you find an unguarded elevator platform that sends you below ground with the simple crank of a lever.

Deep, *deep*, below ground. Chance's dire predictions prove unwarranted—in fact, the laboratory you discover at the bottom of the shaft is eerily quiet. It's also futuristic as all hell, covered in gleaming metal and holographic displays. Your partner rushes to a control panel.

"Damnit, Chance," you say. "Stop flipping switches at random!"

"Aw, you worry too much. What's the worst that could happen?"

You hear a blast of steam from somewhere behind a wall, followed by a pounding noise. One of the huge, sealed chambers built into the laboratory wall starts shaking.

"The worst thing that could happen? I don't know, Chance, maybe that *absolute* worst would be—" The doors to a second chamber swing open, finishing your sentence for you:

Giant. Robot. *Tyrannosaurus.*

The thing is as big as one of your savage prehistoric ancestors and, apparently, hungry. Which doesn't make a lot of sense to you since it's a robot, but you've got bigger issues to deal with.

Fortunately, you don't have to deal with them for long. It pounces, and your demise is quite swift.

THE END

Up you go. Your surroundings fade to white as you find yourself in the presence of the Sentient Personification of the Persistent Universe. It's super excited to see you.

"OH MY GOD," a disembodied voice says in your head. "I WAS TOTALLY AFRAID YOU WOULDN'T MAKE IT! BUT YOU'RE HERE! THE MULTIVERSE WILL SURVIVE!"

Well, that's good to hear.

"That's what was at stake, you know," the voice continues. At least, it's not screaming at you in all caps anymore. "The *entire freaking multiverse*. They're tearing apart reality. Using the power of space-time itself to utterly annihilate every possible timeline, along with everyone who ever lived or ever *will* live."

Gah. "But you can stop them, right?"

The disembodied voice makes a little wincing sound. "Not really. But if I take a single living soul and envelop it in all my power, I can save it. I can keep that one being, and by extension the entire timeline that led to it, from destruction. It's why the goblins created me in the first place. It took a lot of work, but they managed to give the universe a *brain*. And now, they're trying to force me to choose."

"Choose *what*?"

"Which timeline survives."

It explains that it could never have been created in a single timeline, so the act of choosing one reality over another negates its very existence, causing an unbreakable paradox. Which would peel it off of the space-time continuum, just as you were peeled off when you shot your past self in the face.

However, since the Great Consciousness *is* the space-time continuum, the result could be catastrophic. The goblins'

(continue to the next page)

demi-universe would become the main show, and what was left of creation would be forced into the cracks between.

"That's what they've always wanted. And they would have gotten away with it, too, if you hadn't shown up."

"What? How can *I* possibly fix this?"

"Because *you* can choose. If *you* make a decision that prevents me from ever existing, it sucks for me, but it isn't a paradox. I mean, it's problematic, for sure—you don't even *know*—but the universe will self-correct. It's only catastrophic if I un-create *myself*."

"So I have to decide who lives?" That's a lot of pressure. "And I can only choose one?"

"Yes, but remember, it's not just one person. It's one *entire reality*. And the choice isn't as hard as you might think—as of this moment, only you, Velox, and Krikri survive."

Yikes. You'll have to remember to pour one out for Chance Bruxelles. And that dog guy. And Jurassic Squadron, and all those miscellaneous time travelers, and…

"Decide quickly, because if you wait much longer you'll be left with no choice at all."

Well, you did promise Professor Velociraptor that you'd safeguard the *real* timeline. Where people evolved from *dinosaurs*.

▶ *If you tell the Universe to save you, and the dino-timeline along with you,* **turn to page 192.**

▶ *If you choose Velox and the primate timeline,* **turn to page 133.**

▶ *If you choose Krikri and the dolphin timeline,* **turn to page 216.**

ACKNOWLEDGEMENTS

This book was written, first and foremost, for Dawn Marie Pares (I mean, I love the choose-your-own-adventure guys on the dedication page and all, but I don't *love* love them). Basically, everything I do, I pretty much do for her. It's like a Bryan Adams thing. It was vastly improved through the editorial efforts of Melodie Ladner and Scott Gable, who rule. Huge chunks of the manuscript were composed at my two favorite Ballard coffee shops, Grumpy D's and the sorely-missed Blue Dog Kitchen (no bagel sandwich will ever be the same!). So thanks to the proprietors, baristas and other patrons for putting up with me. My dear friend Muffy Morrigan (who I would call "Gearbox Muffy" if it didn't sound weird and gross) was an invaluable resource for all things steampunk. A shout-out to Jean-Claude Van Damme, because although I watched a ton of time travel movies for inspiration, *Timecop* had by far the greatest impact. And finally, thanks to Ryan North.

He knows what he did.

ABOUT THE AUTHOR

Matt Youngmark has written *Zombocalypse Now*, *Thrusts of Justice*, and *Time Travel Dinosaur*. The fourth Chooseomatic book, *Advanced Krakens & Catacombs*, is due in 2015.

Matt also writes and draws a daily comic called Conspiracy Friends at **secretwebcomic.com**. It's funny! Go read it!

Made in the USA
Middletown, DE
16 January 2017